THE MARKS LEFT ON HER

PRAISE FOR THE MARKS LEFT ON HER

'This novel is a must-read for all survivors of sexual assault who want to find community and peace through Di's strength and courage.'

Jessica Morgan, Refinery29 UK

'Powerful read. I felt like she was taking me on a train through her journey while sitting right by.'

Nilly Naseer-Farooqui, Human Rights Advocate

'Di weaves a literary masterpiece as she tells her heart-wrenching story with remarkable delicacy. It is beautiful, painful, and I have yet to recover.'

Reni K Amayo, Author of 'Daughters of Nri'

'An exceptional insight into trauma, identity and life as a woman living outside the bounds of society's gaze.'

WCAN

THE MARKS LEFT ON HER

DI LEBOWITZ

ONWE

ONWE

First published in Great Britain in 2021 by Onwe Press Ltd

This hardback edition was first published in 2021

1 3 5 7 9 10 8 6 4 2

A CIP catalogue record for this book is available from the British Library.

eBook ISBN 978-1-913872-01-4
Hardback ISBN 978-1-913872-00-7

Printed and bounded by Clays Ltd, Elcograf S.p.A.

FSC
www.fsc.org
MIX
Paper from
responsible sources
FSC® C018072

www.onwe.co | @weareonwe

To the women who raised me.

PROLOGUE

For almost a decade I was unable to talk to anyone let alone myself about what I had dubbed 'The Incident', the consequences of which called into question my memory, my sanity and my entire being to the point where I had begun to think of myself as a 'Mad Woman Lost'—some deranged woman gone astray. It took almost ten years to finally admit to myself what had happened to me, and even to this day I still struggle with something that echoes of taboo, shame and guilt.

Flash forward to two years ago, over coffee above Waterloo station with my close friend A.W., I was asked a question that would be the catalytical motivation for writing this book. She asked, 'Why does their learning have to involve our pain?' By 'their' A.W. meant the men that have left footprints or even craters on our lives.

Those poignant words lingered within for days as I realised that I had no way to answer that question. I simply didn't know and that bothered me. It bothered me like the itchy lace bra strap that digs into your body, which has in turn been told constantly that it would never be perfect, nor even satisfactory. It bothered me like the agonising uterine ache that you get when you're on your period, while your male boss doesn't quite get why you 'need a minute' to breathe through the pain with a clenched smile. It bothered me.

So, what began as an attempt to answer A.W.'s question became a means to self-examine, to find a way to purge myself of the events that led up to and that followed 'The Incident'. This grew almost organically into a collection of scribbled-down memories that had been burrowed deep within. Those memories eventually formed the story which you are about to read.

All of these stories are based on true events of my life starting from Hong Kong, then to Paris, Cumbria and finally London. Every effort has been made to portray actual events accurately, but they are nonetheless based on my memory. Where specific details of events could not be recalled, I hope to convey their emotional truth to preserve the story's authenticity. All names of people mentioned in this book have been changed to protect their identities.

Our main character is unnamed, and this was a deliberate choice. There are so many girls and women out there who suffer or have suffered and survived that do not get named. This book is for them—the innumerable unnamed girls and women—so that you may know and be reminded you are not alone.

MY TAILORED PERSON-SUIT

I don't recall when I put it on—
this person-suit
Was it when I was a child
when I concealed rage
and disappointment?
Or was it something that grew
on top of me,
around me,
engulfing me—
a scrim of personhood
now a thick coat of
pretence?
I'm trying to find the zip
to take this person-suit off.
But I'm having difficulty.
I look in crooks
and armpits
of my soul and psyche
and come to realise that
this person-suit
has been stitched on,
sewn over and woven into
who I once was.
My tailored person-suit.

A NOTE ABOUT THE LANGUAGE

Part 1 takes place in pre-1997 Hong Kong during which Hong Kong's official languages were Cantonese and English. Both are the girl's native tongues. It should be noted that when the girl converses with her mother, her Auntie Yin or her peers at school, she is speaking in English. Anytime when the girl or any of her family members converse with her grandmother—her Paupau—it should be assumed that these conversations are conducted in Cantonese.

The girl's Paupau does not speak formal Cantonese but rather a unique combination of the Hakka dialect, her native tongue, and the Ping Chau dialect, a variant of Cantonese deriving from Tung Ping Chau Island. Every effort has been made to preserve Paupau's unique way of speaking when translating this into English.

PART I

The greatest thing about being a child? The adults had all the answers. You never really needed to worry.

ONE

MR OILY MAN

Her bag was heavy, so heavy that it weighed her down. Pink damp towel wrapped around a partially wrung chlorine-infused swimming costume, spilling out for all the world to see. Small steps made clumsier by stubby, tanned legs. Ballerinas were meant to be graceful and poised but not this seven-year-old. Her wet hair latched onto her sunburnt back making large tentacles of water stains across her oversized neon green T-shirt. Her mother had walked far ahead. Bag here. Bag there. Cheap plastic bags with frayed edges, imprinted with 'Morning Star Travel Agent' in faded white on the side.

'Mummy, wait for me. My bag is so heavy. Wait for me, Mummy. Please. You're walking too fast!' the girl cried out.

But her mother had already crossed the busy street and was now waiting on the other side by the tram stop, unaware that her daughter hadn't managed to catch up. Neither mother nor daughter noticed that someone else had been following the girl as she dragged her bag awkwardly towards the traffic lights. Someone was now standing much too close to the girl with his giant shadow casting over her as if to engulf her entirely. Gold teeth lined up along crooked yellow ones. Slicked-back black oily hair. A musty, waxy smell: artificial coconut.

'Aren't you a pretty little girl!' Grinning at her, the man stroked her forearm, his fingernails scratching at the surface of her skin whilst he stared straight at her. His breath on her face stank of putrid rotten spirits. Repugnant. She felt her guts recoil.

'Don't be shy, you pretty thing. I don't bite.'

Fingers crawling on her shoulder, then a hand on the small of her back. Tiny invasions, her territory occupied just the same. Everything inside her told her to scream, to push him away, to kick, to hit, to do something. But she just stood there, frozen. Her legs pathetic, useless, like ice cream cones that have melted into the cement pavement. She simply could not lift them. Her voice that so frequently deafened anyone that came too close to her favourite chocolate treats was now mute.

Green lights! Run! Run! Run! She dashed across the street, sprinting at full speed, lunging towards her mother as she wrapped her arms around her.

'Hey! Don't run so fast across the street! It's not safe, you can trip. Not safe.'

The girl didn't care that her mother scolded her. All she knew was that now she actually was safe because her mother would protect her from Mr Oily Man.

'Where is your bag?' Her mother's brows narrowed. The girl's stomach turned upside down. *Oh no! My bag!* She had left it on the other side of the street, next to Mr Oily Man, and dreaded the thought that her mother would make her walk back to collect it. To the girl's surprise, her mother didn't make her retrieve her bag. Perhaps it was a mother's instinct that kicked in as they watched Mr Oily Man's perverted smirk change to a sheepish frown, or perhaps it was the girl's pale face or her shaking body that alarmed her mother. Whatever it was, the mother grabbed the girl firmly by one arm and stomped their way back across the street, glaring at Mr Oily Man the entire time. She picked up the girl's bag and flung it across the other arm, still glaring at the man, then whirled around in choreographed disgust, her daughter gazing at her with gratitude, and stomped back.

'Are you okay?' Her mother's voice was now gentle.

'Ah-huh. I'm okay, Mummy. I'm sorry I left the bag back there.' The girl looked at the floor.

'No sorry. Nothing to be sorry for.' Her mother brushed the girl's hair away from her face. 'That man, did he say something to you to scare you?' That was her chance, her chance to tell her mother about Mr Oily Man, about his hands on her and his sordid smile.

'No, Mummy.'

'Are you sure?'

'Ah-huh,' the girl nodded timidly.

Seated on the lower deck of the tram heading home, the girl couldn't help but replay what had happened with Mr Oily Man over and over again in her head. Goosebumps up and down her arm as she shivered.

'Put this on.'

Her mother wrapped a cardigan around the girl, thinking the summer breeze was too chilly for her. If only her mother had known they were shudders of fear. *Why didn't I tell Mummy? I should tell Mummy. That man. He wasn't a nice man. He made me feel bad. He made me scared. I should tell Mummy he was scary. I should tell Mummy.*

The girl never did, not even to this day.

TWO

MONSTERS UNDER THE BED

The corner of the bag was poking out, a thick crumpled black paper bag with a glossy finish. Thick gold ribbons stretched horizontally across the opening, tied shut with black shoelace tips. It was the kind of bag you'd get when you bought something expensive, from somewhere fancy and Western. The kind of bag you'd get handed to you by immaculate manicured hands and a lipsticked smile. It was the kind of bag you wouldn't expect to find under the king-sized bed which the girl shared with her mother, draped with faded pink worn-out sheets dotted with lint bobbles and matching pillows.

'Never look under bed. Under bed, not for you. Things inside for Mummy only. They are Mummy things. Only for Mummy, not for you, okay?' her mother had warned her one day, not realising that as soon as you tell a child never to look at something, the prohibition would only fuel a child's curiosity.

The girl would come to understand that her mother had secrets she wanted to keep from the girl, secrets which the girl had to assume were probably more horrific than any other monster that lurks under beds. At eight years old, the girl had a handle on monsters under beds, at least in her imagination, but she wasn't entirely sure what 'secrets' even were except that they were things you couldn't share or show, things that were forbidden. Forbidden meant thrilling.

One night when the girl's mother was at work, the 'secret' was poking out from under the bed in the form of the fancy paper bag. It seemed to be exposing itself, luring the girl to satisfy her curiosity. She happened, fortunately or not, to be alone. Paupau had gone to bed and Auntie Yin was in her room studying hard. This was her chance and she took it.

Squatting over the corner of the bag, her hands began to shake nervously. She closed her eyes as she tugged at the corner of the bag—fearing to rip it—and out slid a magazine. *Oooh! Magazine!* She loved magazines for their big bright pictures and the glossy paper. She read the title and spelt it out in her head. *H-U-S-T-L-E-R.* The cover looked nothing like anything she had seen before. *This woman has no clothes on.* As soon as she flipped the magazine open, she understood the true meaning of secrets. Secrets were things that made your face go red like watermelon flesh. Secrets were things you don't dare speak aloud because they carried with it a stench like stinky tofu sold by street hawkers on a humid April afternoon. Secrets were bad things you keep from other people because they are too shameful to show others. Secrets were things you don't even tell Mr Father Lam at confession on Sunday morning before Mass because they were too terrifying.

Her eyes were too afraid to look at what she already knew was there, but she looked anyway, she couldn't help it. Images upon images of women. Flesh upon flesh, lots and lots of flesh. Women, men, breasts, private parts all glistening and moist. She couldn't comprehend why those images both disgusted and intrigued her as she frenziedly flicked over page after page until she stopped at the centrefold. The woman was completely naked, perched against a bed with her legs spread wide apart, exposing herself entirely. Her hand with manicured red claws was touching herself as she stared straight at the girl. This woman was smiling unashamedly. *Why is she smiling?*

The girl suddenly thought about what her Paupau taught her about a woman's nakedness, about sin, shame, guilt and Eve.

'Cannot be naked. Ay-yah. Woman naked so shameful, so sinful! Very bad. You see, Eve—she first woman. She very disobedient to Mr God, no clothing, just naked. Mr God punished her and made her put clothes on.' Her Paupau's warning ran through her mind.

Suddenly she felt as if the naked woman was really able to see her, and the girl slammed the magazine shut. She quickly looked up at the door, petrified she may have been caught, but no one was there. *Phew*. Then she looked up at the crucifix above her mother's vanity table and wondered if He had been watching.

'Mr God always watching. He see you. You good girl, He see. You bad girl, He see. You lazy, He see. You lie, He see. He see everything. God always watching everything. Cannot hide,' her Paupau would warn her.

It unnerved her that God had just witnessed her rooting out her mother's secrets. She would later wonder if God would tell on her (was He a snitch?), but for now her mind was invaded by a swarm of more pressing questions. She didn't understand why her mother would have such a shocking magazine in the first place. She wondered if her mother had also seen the same stark pictures, and if she had, why in the world was she keeping them around? *Why does Mummy have this? Paupau said being naked is bad. It's wrong like Eve. She was naked and she was bad, so God punished her and made her put clothes on. Is Mummy bad? Am I bad? Why does Mummy have this?* The girl couldn't come to terms with what she had seen. It planted seeds of doubt in the girl's impression of her mother.

The girl never looked under the bed ever again, for she was petrified of what else she would discover. There were monsters all right, just not the kind in fairy tales.

THREE

SWIM OR DIE

Ever since her mother was a child, she had been an avid swimmer. By her mother's late teens, her talent was documented by photographs of stunt-like back dives off a pier into the open sea. More impressive were her competitions in the Hong Kong cross-harbour races. Up until 1978, thousands of swimmers had flocked to Hong Kong's rather narrow but deep harbour for its annual cross-harbour races. So, it was only natural that when it was time for the girl to learn how to swim, her mother had great expectations. Mother-daughter Sunday afternoons splashing, swimming, diving, perhaps at some point in the open sea. Her mother beamed with excitement at the prospect of an activity they could bond over, but as was the case with so many little Hong Kong girls, disappointing one's mother for not meeting expectations was just part of the mother-daughter dynamic.

The girl couldn't swim. She could barely float, but that did not stop her from diving headfirst into a swimming pool, twice. The first time the girl was only five—that wonderful age when a child knows no fear of anything, let alone of injury or of death.

It was probably the girl's first pool birthday party at one of her friend's homes who lived in Tai Koo Shing—an expensive private residential development that catered to Hong Kong's emerging middle class and its many recent Japanese immigrants.

Watching her friends hurtling joyfully into the pool, the girl decided, whimsically, carelessly, blithely ignorant, that it would be fun to do the same. But it was not. Not at all. If anything, it taught her two vital lessons. The first was that she was definitely not a fish nor a mermaid—an important reality check for a girl so convinced that the Little Mermaid was real. And second was that her mother knew how to fix any problem, including how to jump into a kiddie pool fully clothed to fish her daughter out, and also how to perform CPR.

Fearful that her daughter would sooner or later plunge herself to death in a paddling pool, the girl's mother decided it was time to enrol her daughter on a swimming class. Her mother had been eager to teach her daughter herself. After all, who could have been better to teach swimming than a cross-harbour competitor? But after two traumatic instances of 'let's just dive in and see what happens', her mother decided against it and thought it would be less overwhelming to leave the education to the professionals.

'This is my daughter. She is here for the class.' Her mother pushed the girl forward to greet her new swim coach.

A short and very tanned middle-aged man with a jagged smile approached the girl.

'Hello! Why, aren't you an adorable pretty girl!' Mr Swim Coach leant towards the girl and squeezed her cheek. She hated the unwelcome contact but had been taught to be polite and smile. 'Such a cute half-caste girl! Don't worry, she looks very clever. Look at those big *guai-mui* eyes. We'll get her swimming in no time.'

Stale cigarette breath wafted over her nostrils as Mr Swim Coach led the girl over to the children's pool and slid into the pool.

'Okay. Come on, jump in. Don't worry, it's not deep. You can stand on the bottom.' Mr Swim Coach waved for her to get in with him and the rest of children. The girl approached right to the fringe of the pool and looked down. *Hmmm. Doesn't look that scary, I guess,* she thought to herself anxiously, toes gripping onto the edge until they turned pale. She felt uneasy; the last two times she dove straight into a pool, she nearly drowned.

'Come on. Don't waste my time,' shouted Mr Swim Coach.

Like any dutiful, respectful student, she did what she was told and jumped in. Big splash! Emerging from the water, she was all smiles as she tiptoed along the bottom. *I'm okay. This is nice. I like this! I can do this*, she thought to herself as she joined the other novices in learning how to kick their legs back whilst holding onto the edge of the pool. As she kicked the water with her chubby legs, she imagined herself as a synchronised swimmer, gliding across a gigantic pool gracefully. *I'm going to be a better swimmer than Ariel in no time.* Childish fantasies.

'Okay, class. Let's now practise how to control our breath underwater and float at the same time,' instructed Mr Swim Coach as he gestured for an older student to approach and demonstrate. It looked so easy. The boy took a deep breath, placed himself flat-faced on top of the water and started blowing bubbles. The girl was astounded at how the boy floated effortlessly. *Wow! I want to blow bubbles. Cool bubbles!* The girl couldn't wait to get started.

After a few more demonstrations, the other children were quickly grasping how to float on water. The girl just stood and watched; she was still anxious about choking again. Noticing she was struggling, Mr Swim Coach said he would help her. As instructed, she took a deep breath and placed her face onto the surface of the water. *Huh? Why isn't this working? I'm not floating.* No bubble-blowing skills.

'Stop. Stop. Stop. I'll help you. Do the same again. I'll give you a hand.'

So, she did. Mr Swim Coach's hands on her upper thighs. *I'm doing it! I'm floating!* Mr Swim Coach's slippery hands slithering up to her tummy. *Don't touch my tummy.* Mr Swim Coach's unfamiliar, unwelcomed hands sliding all over her. *No! Don't. Yuck! No!* Panicked, she kicked as hard as she could for Mr Swim Coach to stop. Immediately he let go of the girl, who was now gasping for air as she began to gulp water. Still kicking, she felt the familiar sensation of inhaling chorine water; coughing, choking. *Help. Help! Mummy!* Big arms lifted her effortlessly out of the water, though not out of danger; surprise surprise, it was Mr Swim Coach.

'Why did you kick me, silly girl?! You kicked me very hard! I was trying to help you, to teach you! You silly girl!'

The girl was too afraid to shout back at him although she really wanted to. She wanted to scream in his face but didn't quite fathom the extent of her rage. All she knew was that she had this awful feeling that something was horribly wrong when his hands glided over and grabbed at her. She said nothing. She did nothing. She simply looked up at Mr Swim Coach with her bloodshot eyes from the chlorine and the choking. The other children were watching. Some giggled and laughed at the girl. Some were baffled, uncomfortable. Some, doubtless, understood.

When it was time to be picked up, she could not have been more relieved for a class to be over. As soon as she got a glimpse of her mother, she sprinted towards her, clamped on, and squeezed as hard as she could, hoping she could wring out what had happened. Her mother knew instantly something was off because the girl had never been a clingy child. Something was definitely not right.

'Erh . . . How was she? Did she do okay?' quizzed her mother, eyebrows close together, concerned eyebrows.

'Well . . . She was okay. She is quite afraid of water. She doesn't know how to float yet . . . I think she had a bit of a scare.' Mr Swim Coach's yellow-toothed smile concealed the truth.

'Oh. Really?'

She looked at her daughter, her eyes searching for an explanation for the girl's uncharacteristic behaviour.

'No, Mummy. I . . . I choked again, like last time.'

She tugged at her mother, tears trickling down her face.

'What? What happened?' asked her mother, who was surprised and confused. She didn't understand why her daughter had such an exaggerated response to a habitat that she herself considered so natural. But the girl continued to cry as she hid behind her mother's arms.

'I guess she's still scared from the last two times. You know she almost drowned. Must still be afraid.'

Her mother was more apologetic than concerned, as if she were embarrassed that her daughter had made such a big show out of an unsuccessful swimming lesson.

'Erm, I'm sorry, Coach. Maybe next time.'

No, Mummy. He touched me. I didn't like it. I don't like him. I had to kick. I got scared and I choked. No, Mummy. Don't call him. Don't bring me back here. No, Mummy. Please.

Those are the words she wished she had said to her mother, but she never did.

After the girl's extreme reactions to her failed swimming lesson, the mother decided it best to leave the subject altogether alone for a couple of years. During that time, the girl taught herself how to doggy paddle, float and blow bubbles underwater—all sufficient skills to help her survive in water that reached above her head. Her inability to mermaid-slither her way up and down pool lanes did not stop her enthusiasm for anything water-related, especially her frequent visits to Hong Kong's only fully operational aqua theme park, Water World. It was a magical and beloved place of escape for Hong Kongers of all ages from the swelteringly humid summers.

At Water World, she arm-banded herself up and flung herself down slides, through tunnels, dashed down water obstacle courses and even braved the simulated wave pool. So long as she had her trusty arm bands, she was invincible!

Her confidence appeased her mother's worries enough to allow the girl to go to Victoria Park Public Swimming Pool with her Auntie Yin. She had never gone swimming with Auntie Yin before. In fact, apart from their weekly Friday night ice-cream trips up the road, the girl had never gone anywhere with just her Auntie Yin before. It would be their first solo trip together. The girl was both nervous and excited.

Auntie Yin was her mother's youngest sister and had lived with the family since before the girl was born. To the girl, Auntie Yin was more like the older sister that she never had whom she looked up to not only because of her Auntie's extremely high intelligence, but for her stubborn dedication to bettering herself through education. It was through this dedication that Auntie Yin managed to become the first member in their entire extended family to enter university and would later inspire the girl's love for learning, books and school.

Auntie Yin epitomised independence and self-efficiency. Whilst she loved her little niece very much, she firmly believed that mollycoddling or pandering to her was not good. As far as Auntie Yin was concerned, being eight years old was old enough for the girl to be allocated HKD$1, to find a locker, work out how to use it and be responsible for her own locker key.

'I'm not your mother. You are old enough to figure it out yourself. You can read, can't you? So read the instructions, follow them and you can do it yourself.'

It was the first time the girl had ever been spoken to with such candour and she loved it! *Auntie Yin doesn't treat me like a little girl or talk to me like I am stupid. Auntie Yin gives me stuff to do for myself. I love this!* She was beside herself with her first taste of adulthood. It took the girl a good five minutes to work out how to operate the locker, but when she did, she was ecstatic. *I did it! I didn't need any help and I did it! I can do stuff!*

She was still giddy as they headed outside to the swimming pools. The floor had been baking under the mid-July sun and as soon as the girl took her first step onto the scorching tiles, she realised she had forgotten her flip-flops. *I can use my ballet skills!* she thought to herself as she tried to skip and dart behind her Auntie. But it was of little use. Each hot-potato step felt like it should be accompanied with a sizzle sound which she played in her head. *Sizz. Sizz. Ouch. Sizz. Ouch. Hot! Hot! Ouch.*

'I'm sorry you forgot your flip-flops but I'm not going to lend you mine. You need to learn the consequences of your actions, or lack of actions. If you forget things, you need to deal with what happens. It's called being independent. Don't want to forget? Learn to pack your bag the night before and check it twice,' lectured Auntie Yin in her usual matter-of-fact stoic manner.

Those words of wisdom still resonate to this day. As a woman she still packed her bag the night before, sometimes even weeks in advance, checking and re-checking, to be sure nothing was forgotten.

'Come. Sit down here.' Auntie Yin signalled to her to sit by the very adult, very scary Olympic-sized pool, right up at the deep end, the five-metre-deep end. It was so deep that the water was a dark turquoise and made the pool look bottomless. The girl took a huge gulp.

'You see those people swimming, yes? Those people know how to swim. Like this lady,'—Auntie Yin pointed at a slender Hong Kongese woman around her Auntie's age who glided across the water like a pro—'she is a very good swimmer. Pick someone, watch how they swim.'

The girl looked around at the heads bobbing in and out of the water. She wasn't sure what made someone a good swimmer so decided to stick with the same woman her Auntie had pointed out.

'You picked someone?' asked her Auntie.

The girl nodded her head eagerly.

'Okay. Good. You stay here. You don't move and you watch them swim. I'll come back in an hour.'

Before she could ask Auntie Yin what the purpose of this observational exercise was, her Auntie had already turned around and shuffled off. The girl was too afraid to stand up and chase after her as that would entail disobeying what she was tasked to do. So, the dutiful niece sat cross-legged and watched the woman she had picked swim up and down and when she got out of the pool and left, the girl picked out another person and repeated the process.

The sun had been beating down on the girl for what felt like hours and her back began to feel like suckling pig crackling. Restless, the girl's mind began to wander and daydream. *This is getting boring. I wonder when Auntie Yin will be back. My back hurts. It feels really hot. I'm thirsty. I wanna Coke. I'm hungry. Noodles. Yes. Noodles after swimming. I wonder if Auntie Yin will take me to that beef brisket noodle shop next door . . . Yum! I wonder if Paupau is cooking dinner yet. Maybe it will be beef with garlic sauce. Yum . . .*

'You ready?' Auntie Yin was back and had interrupted the girl's daydream of her favourite dishes lined up across endless dining tables.

'Umm, yes . . .?' She said yes but had no clue as to what she was supposed to be ready for.

'Okay. Stand up. Put on your goggles.'

The girl did as was instructed.

'Now put your toes on the edge of the swimming pool.'

Again, the girl followed.

'Look down. You see how deep the water is? Yes? Very deep, yes?'

SPLASH! Frantic paddling, head bobbing up and down, arms trying to grab at something that wasn't there. The all-too-familiar feeling of inhaling water as the girl's arms flapped about hysterically. Heart beating wildly out of her chest. *It's too deep. I'm going to drown. Auntie Yin! Auntie Yin! WHY DID YOU PUSH ME IN? How could you? Help! Help!* But those thoughts were just that, thoughts.

'Swim! You must swim!' Auntie Yin called out to her, confident in her niece.

The girl managed to doggy paddle and keep her head up out of the water but the panic of almost drowning had exhausted her. Her legs began to lose their strength as she looked up to her Auntie Yin, her eyes begging her Auntie to come and rescue her.

'I cannot swim! I don't know how to swim! You were studying! Now SWIM! You swim or you die! Swim!' exclaimed Auntie Yin.

The sheer roar of her conviction that her niece would swim had a miraculous effect because suddenly the girl understood no one was going to come and save her, that she was going to have to save herself. As if by magical willpower, the girl managed to muster the strength in her arms and legs to start doggy paddling in order to keep her head above the water. Slowly, the girl began to move her arms and legs in a semi-synchronised breaststroke manner, something like what she had observed the other swimmers do for so long that day, as she bobbed towards the side of the pool and latched onto the nearest edge. *I didn't drown. I didn't die. I did it. I'm not drowning. I can do this! Yes. I can do this!* The girl was still digesting the shock but at the same time was filled with a sense of pride she had never felt before.

'See. What did I say? You can swim. Why need swimming lessons? No need. You're a smart girl, you can work it out yourself.' Auntie Yin smiled.

After a few minutes, the girl caught her breath and decided to give her semi-synchronised breaststroke a try again—although she was sure to stay right up against the edge of the pool just in case. The girl would go on to perfect her swimming technique with every trip to the pool until she was able to swim lengths of Olympic-sized pools as well as the open sea without hesitation.

Since that day, the girl learnt a vital lesson that she carries with her even now: when you're drowning and screaming for help, no one is going to come and rescue you. You have to save yourself.

FOUR

POOLSIDE BAGELS

Mr Harry was her mother's special friend and the girl's first solid memory of what a father figure would be like. The girl didn't know much about Mr Harry except that he must have been very wealthy to afford several business trips from New York to Hong Kong each year and stay at the lavishly luxurious Regent Hotel right by the harbour in Tsim Sha Tsui—a highly urbanised area dense with five-star hotels, designer boutiques, bustling nightlife and modern shopping malls.

The girl loved Mr Harry's visits to Hong Kong not just because he always greeted her with a warm jolly smile and a thick New York accent that made him sound like a character from a film, but because his visits meant invitations to join him for lavish buffet dinners and being treated to fancy hotel chocolate wrapped in expensive gold paper.

Mr Harry doted affection on the girl as a father would dote on his daughter upon his return from trips abroad with extravagant gifts she could only dream about: a pair of black suede ballerina pumps embellished with pretty pink and yellow flowers from a high-end shoe retailer, La Saunda, that she had coveted for months, a bright pink sewing machine, a life-sized doll that talked every time you kissed her (which after watching *Child's Play* was quickly relegated to the deepest part of her wardrobe), and all the dark chocolate truffles the girl could eat.

Each time she saw Mr Harry, he would have a surprise for her, and each time when she asked why she was given such a wonderful present, he always told that her it was for being 'such a good girl'. Many years later, the girl would come to realise that Mr Harry's generous kindness was not just out of his affection for her mother. Rather he had taken pity on the girl whose own father had long abandoned her.

But it wasn't just the presents or buffet dinners that the girl looked forward to. Her favourite part about Mr Harry's visits was whenever he would invite her and her mother over on a Sunday to spend the afternoon at the Regent's fancy outdoor swimming pool. The girl was so thrilled at the invitation that she spent Saturday evening conscientiously packing her bag with her nicest sports outfit, her swimming suit, goggles, suntan lotion, hairbrush and other bits and bobs one might find in a typical eight-year-old's bag.

On her very first visit, she felt dwarfed by the awesome size of the hotel. *Wow! This place is huge!* The girl thought as her eyes tried to grasp the sheer size of the hotel lobby. Everything looked, smelt, and felt different. Everything was so clean, so bright, so smart. *This floor is so shiny and clean I can see my reflection! Wow!* The girl thought she had stepped into a palace—one that could only be frequented by the Westerners who could afford it. It was a stark contrast from the types of places locals would visit; places with their overpowering smell of cigarettes, street-food and questionable hygiene levels.

As soon as the girl saw the kidney-shaped pool she realised she was in very unfamiliar territory. Unlike Victoria Park Swimming Pool, this one didn't have an overpowering chlorine odour. The dark green mould that grew on the edges of so many public swimming pools she had been in, that mould which made her skin curl and cringe, wasn't there. There was no mould, just perfectly bleached white tiles. It looked like something out of a travel magazine.

The place sounded different too. Instead of Cantonese— a language the girl heard almost all of the time except at school—she could only hear perfect English being spoken. *Everyone is speaking English. They can all speak English like me.* This made the girl feel more comfortable until she noticed several other children playing in the pool. Although they shared similar features with their lightly tanned bronze skin, big round eyes and stocky frame, the girl couldn't help but notice something about her and the other children was different. These children wore swimming costumes in all sorts of bright fashionable colours and patterns. Costumes that made her feel a strange sensation that felt so alien to her. She was suddenly very aware that she didn't quite belong with the other children but didn't know why. As she looked down at her thin cheap costume with the faded garish patterns and colours, she wondered for the first time what being different meant, and why she was so different from the other children despite looking just like them. She decided to shrug off her thoughts and just enjoy splashing about in the pool.

After a couple of hours of swimming, the girl grew hungry but was too nervous to pipe up like she usually did.

'Mummy, I'm . . . I'm, um, hungry,' she whispered to her mother sheepishly.

Her mother scrunched her face, uncertain as to why her daughter had suddenly decided to play timid. Her mother gestured to Mr Harry for them to have lunch to appease her daughter's appetite and they made their way to the poolside restaurant.

The whole setup was like a film. It amazed the girl. Before she could even realise what was happening, the waiters arrived, laid down starched white tablecloths, silverware, crystal glasses, serviettes all around and even draped her in a fluffy white bathrobe.

'This is for Miss. We don't want you catching a cold now, do we?' said the headwaiter.

As she wrapped herself up, she thought, *I love this! This is like being in* Annie, *only better because I'm in it! Wow! Mr Harry must be a very important man.*

But then the nervousness kicked in again. She couldn't make sense of the menu. It was in English but abundant with food she had never heard of. She searched the menu for something familiar. *Where's the squid and fish ball noodles?*

Where's the pineapple bun and milk tea? Mr Harry must have read the girl's look of concern, for as if on cue, he asked the very question that would change her gastronomic life for ever.

'Have you ever tried a bagel?' Mr Harry asked in his thick New York accent.

'No . . . erm, what's a bagel?' She puckered her lips in consternation at the menu, curious about this bagel-sounding thing.

'Well, my dear, a bagel is the best thing you can ever have. It's like bread and like a doughnut but better! And I always, always, get it with smoked salmon and cream cheese. You'll love it!'

This was precisely why she came to love her afternoons with Mr Harry—he was able to teach her things about a world that she could never access through her mother, Paupau or anyone else.

'Okay! Can I have a bagel, please? And . . . a chocolate milkshake! And onion rings!'

The girl wasn't even sure if they were on the menu but was so excited that she couldn't help but keep adding to her order.

'That's my girl! Your daughter's got such a great appetite! It's great.' Mr Harry laughed.

She had never been called 'my girl' by someone outside of her family before and certainly not by a man of her father's age. She felt warm and tingly, the same feeling she would get just before blowing her candles out on her birthday cake.

Sat at the fanciest outside dining table, at the fanciest pool, at the fanciest hotel, she had her first bagel experience. Lightly toasted onion bagel, slightly crispy on the outside yet chewy and soft on the inside. Smothered with cold cream cheese, lined with smoked salmon, topped with sour capers and finished off with thin shavings of sweet red onion. Mr Harry had introduced her to her very first taste of typical Jewish deli food and it would be a comfort food to her throughout her life. That first bagel ignited the half-Jewess within her, she just didn't know it at the time.

'So, what do you think? Do you like it?' asked Mr Harry.

'This is A-MAZING!' said the girl, who could barely swallow the bagel fast enough to answer.

Cream cheese smeared all over her face, she beamed the biggest smile she had ever smiled. Mr Harry and her mother chuckled to each other. Who knew such gleeful joy could be found in something as simple as a bagel?

Swinging her legs, gulping her thick chocolate milkshake, wrapped in a fluffy oversized bathrobe, she looked across the table at Mr Harry and her mother. She observed how they looked into each other's eyes and smiled, how the three of them poked fun at each other and roared with laughter. The sight of the three of them together would have appeared perfectly normal to an outsider looking in—a mixed-race daughter with a Western man and Hong Kongese mother. No one would be able to guess that they weren't an actual family, and in that moment the girl enjoyed playing make-believe. She, at that moment, began to value the superficial but genuine comfort of appearances.

For the first time the girl got a glimpse into what it may have been like to have had a father in her life, a father who would teach her how to do water-bomb dives into the pool, how to do a handstand underwater, how to order bagels and how blowing bubbles in her milkshake always made it taste better. For the first time she felt simultaneously ecstatic yet melancholy because she knew those moments would not last, and by the end of the afternoon, she would have to return home to the reality that her real father had left her long ago and wasn't coming back.

FIVE

NO SANTA, I SANTA!

Christmas films. There was nothing more enjoyable than binge-watching seasonal VHS films rented from her local video store, KPS. She adored these films, with their perfectly groomed nuclear families and their excessively large suburban houses. The abundance of sublime snow that she had never seen, dancing and floating from the sky as the backdrop to mulled wine and eggnog sipped by a blazing fireplace. And of course, who could forget Santa Claus—an overweight white man who dished out an obscene number of presents under a six-foot pine tree.

But as the girl got a little older, her beloved films that she had watched and re-watched time and time again caused her much confusion. The picture that was played in her goggle-box was a far cry from the realities of living in a pokey three-bedroom flat cramped amongst the countless high-rise buildings in a residential development in Hong Kong. Her home was not only impossible for Santa to enter, but it seemed every effort had been made to discourage him or anyone else from entering. There were logistical complications that someone from the North Pole might not have anticipated. There was certainly no chimney and the small windows were framed with aluminium bars, which would seem to keep any visitors such as burglars, kidnappers or Santa from climbing in. Before even getting to the front door, one had to bypass the concierge before confronting a metal gate framing their front door. Even if Santa had wanted to pay a visit, he would have been so put off with all that faffing around with locks and metal that he would have probably given up and walked off in a huff.

Then there was the subject of the tree. In her beloved films, the Christmas tree was always a tower of magnificent pine adorned with balls of gold, silver and red, and decorated with detailed ornaments handcrafted with great love and care. Her tree, on the other hand, was three pieces of plastic assembled together and shabbily dressed in cheap tinsel made on the mainland. She didn't know what a pine tree would smell like, but she was certain it wasn't of plastic. All this wasn't helped by the fact that the stories about Santa conflicted directly with the Catholic Christmas story she had also been told, let alone the laws of nature and science themselves. *Why does a fat old white man deliver presents on Mr Jesus' birthday? Shouldn't we give Mr Jesus presents on his birthday? And how can Santa deliver presents to all the children in one night? What about the ones who don't know Santa? Or the ones who don't know Mr Jesus? Did Mr Jesus tell Santa to deliver presents? Maybe he works for Mr Jesus? How much does Mr Jesus pay him? Must be a lot for express delivery.*

What was most confusing about Santa was how her Paupau and her mother had always warned her never, under any circumstances, to allow a stranger to enter their home.

'No stranger. You don't know, you don't let in! Never! Can be bad man, try to hurt you, kidnap you, try to kill you! Never open door to strangers,' her Paupau would warn her.

She was extremely puzzled. *I've never seen Santa. I've never met him. So, Santa's a stranger? So, I can't invite him in? Hmmm. Would that be rude? Paupau says it's very rude not to invite respected elders in for tea and fruit. This is confusing.*

One year when the girl was almost nine, her mother took her to Jusco department store—their local shopping centre just down the road from their flat—for a lazy stroll. For many Hong Kong people, wandering through a shopping mall is a common pastime, particularly during the holidays, and there is no better-loved holiday in Hong Kong than Christmas. Hong Kong <u>loves</u> Christmas, which to an outsider may seem a little surprising considering Hong Kong isn't a particularly Christian city. But it seems when it comes to opportunities for consumerism, no place does it better than Hong Kong.

Feeling especially confident that afternoon, the girl asked her mother if she had told Santa what she wanted for Christmas yet.

'Mummy, did you tell Santa what I want for Christmas yet?' asked the girl.

'What?' Her mother looked baffled and raised an eyebrow.

'You know? For Christmas? Presents? Because I know what I want.'

She was surprised her mother hadn't said anything to Santa. Maybe it was too late. Maybe she won't get anything, or worse still, she hadn't been good enough so there won't be any presents for her after all. Suddenly she felt very anxious.

'What present? No present from Santa.' Her mother shrugged her off.

'What do you mean no present from Santa?' The girl stopped, hands on her hips.

'No Santa. No presents from Santa Claus. He's not giving you presents. No presents.'

Her mother's tone was irked, almost abrasive as she continued walking, the girl now trailing behind.

'But I thought . . . I thought . . .?'

Perplexed, the girl began to shake her head at her mother who was now agitated at her daughter's persistent insistence on presents.

'No Santa. There is no Santa.' Her mother stopped and looked directly at the girl. 'I am Santa. I SANTA CLAUS! I pay for present. Me!' Her mother spat those words at the girl, and each word felt like a slap across the face.

The girl was speechless, stunned, shocked. She stood there frozen in disbelief as she tried to process what her mother had just said. *No Santa? But all the teachers at school talk about Santa and teachers always tell the truth. And the movies talk about Santa. And my friends too. And all the stories. And decorations. And . . . and . . . Were they lying to me? Why would they lie? And you Mummy, you told me about Santa. And now, no Santa? Why do we even have a tree? Can Santa bring me my father for Christmas? What does it all mean?*

For the rest of the afternoon she dragged her feet behind her mother through the shopping centre in silence as she repeated her mother's words over and over in her head. *No Santa! I Santa!* She wanted to query her mother about it again but was too afraid to learn more. She could see the dark circles around her mother's eyes, circles which she had learnt to mean that her mother was not in the best of moods and it would be wise for the girl to be on her best behaviour.

By the time Christmas had arrived, the mother assumed her daughter had forgotten all about those thoughtless words that she had blurted out in a moment of fatigue, but it was too late. Her mother's words could never be unsaid and in that one single afternoon, the girl's childish dreams of Santa, the Tooth Fairy, unicorns and angels were all erased, wiped clean. The girl understood that Santa was make-believe, like all the other whimsical entities she encountered in films and stories. She understood there wasn't a jolly obese white man who would just dish out presents. Understanding that it was all a farce resolved a number of the girl's previous questions about logistics and myths. But what wasn't a farce was that one had to work hard to earn money to purchase presents for spoiled little girls. Her mother worked harder than anyone the girl would ever encounter in her whole life, simply to ensure that every Christmas the girl would have exactly the present she desired, all without the help of any man— Santa, Mr Jesus or otherwise.

Eat your heart out, Santa. We don't need you.

SIX

HOOKING YOUR SOUL OUT

It was coming up on 9:20 p.m. In less than five minutes the girl's Paupau would walk into the bedroom she shared with her mother and remind her that it was time to wash her face, brush her teeth and say her nighttime prayers. It had been the same routine every night for as long as she could remember. Bedtime would not be complete without kneeling on the cool parquet floor and praying to a wooden Mr Jesus crucifix mounted above her mother's black-lacquered vanity table. Whether it was done purposely, or it was simply a coincidence, the crucifix was mounted in such a way that whenever she knelt to pray, she could always catch her reflection in her mother's large mirror, as if a physical reflection of guilt was required to hone in on the Catholic burden of original sin.

Nightly prayers for an eight-year-old was more like a superficial confession followed by a pantomimical petition. Sometimes she felt as if she were talking to the Tooth Fairy or even Santa Claus; her mother had finally straightened those beliefs out. Sometimes she imagined Mr Jesus to be a mystical genie that would grant her wishes of 'world peace' and to 'make everyone happy and good'—all phrases copied and pasted from church, of course. She had no concept of world peace nor what happy nor good really meant, except that they were nice things to wish for. Other times she felt that she needed to 'confess her sins' but was utterly stumped as to what constituted a sin. *Do I count eating too much chocolate ice cream? Does that count? Well, I guess then I should say sorry for that . . . and, ummmm,*

I forgot to put my hand up to ask my teacher to go to the toilet at school today . . . Before she knew it, she was at such a loss as to what to say when praying to Mr God that she began fabricating wishes and sins as if there were some karmic accountant on the other side tallying everything up.

At some point she did learn how to recite the Our Father and the Hail Mary prayers verbatim. She could recite them in both English and Cantonese, switching between languages as she pleased, with no clue as to what any of the words really meant. It made her wonder if Mr God was bilingual like her and if He could also understand other languages too. She knew those prayers had something to do with thanking Mr God and Mrs Mary but got very confused at the idea that Mr God could somehow have a baby called Mr Jesus and that was the same man in marble on the wooden cross who stared down at her every night. What perplexed her even more was how Mr Jesus was also Mr God, but that Mr God was Mr Jesus' father and they both had a special friend in their gang called Mr Holy Spirit. They were all Misters of course, which bugged the girl. She didn't like that there was only one Mrs and that was Mrs Mary who wasn't a part of the special gang called the Holy Trinity. *Pretty cool name for a gang,* she thought. She was fascinated by pictures of Mr Jesus and how he always looked so perfect. Sometimes Mr Jesus was a baby with blonde hair and blue eyes. Other times Mr Jesus was an adult with slightly darker complexion but still considered the epitome of Aryan beauty. *If Mr Jesus was a carpenter, why is his hair so tidy?* She had never seen a picture of Mr God, and when she asked about seeing a picture of Him, she was told that Mr God had no form. She had no clue what that meant but simply accepted the answer. *I guess Mr God doesn't like having his picture taken. Maybe he's shy.*

All those confusing thoughts didn't stop her from following Paupau's strict rule about praying before every bedtime.

Dear Mr Jesus, if you can hear me. . . . Well, I guess you can because Paupau says you're God's son. Umm, if you're God's son, how are you also Mr God? Are you two people? Like my two-in-one shampoo? And Mrs Mary, umm . . . is she married to Mr God? Is she Mrs God? But if you're Mr God too, then is she married to you? But she's your mother? She can't be married to you! Yuck! I'm so sorry! I've got all these questions. I'm really confused, Mr Jesus, because your family tree is . . . confusing. Really, really confusing. I had to draw a family tree at school for homework. It was confusing too. I didn't like doing it. I could write down everyone on Mummy's side but with my dad . . . well . . . it's just my dad, and no one else. I didn't know anyone else to add. I couldn't add . . . I couldn't add any grandparents or aunties or uncles. When my teacher asked where my dad is from, I couldn't say. I think it's America—that's what my Paupau tells me. But she also says I'm Mr Jesus' people. That would be you. What does that mean? I'm so confused. Anyhow, maybe you could tell me one day. Maybe like when I'm sleeping? Maybe you could tell me in a dream? Thank you, Mr God, Mr Jesus and Mrs Mary, for everything. Oh, and yes, world peace and make everything good please! Good night and lots of love, hugs and kisses.

Prefixes were always added to names of adults as it was considered extremely rude to address one's elders simply by their first names unless they were family friends, in which case they would be called Uncle or Auntie so-and-so. Seeing as Mr God, Mr Jesus and Mrs Mary were not family members nor friends of the family, they couldn't be addressed as Uncle God, Uncle Jesus and Auntie Mary—that would be very impolite and her Paupau taught her better than that! The girl accepted her Paupau's etiquette rules as law, but she did always wonder if Mr God was his first or last name, and if it was his first name, was Mr God as special or as famous as Madonna? She did love Madonna after all.

It was now 9:25 p.m. and right on schedule Paupau entered her room to remind her to wash her face, brush her teeth and say her nighttime prayers.

'Already washed. Already brushed, Paupau. Good night,' she reported with pride.

She loved being a step ahead of her Paupau, who held punctuality as a Godly quality which the girl inherited through to adulthood. Her absurd punctuality would later become a nuisance to her loved ones.

'Okay. Nighttime prayers. Must pray, okay? Then switch off bedside light and go sleep,' her Paupau commanded and closed the door.

Ordinarily the girl would have followed suit and gone through the motions of talking to Mr God, but something had gotten into her that night, something she had never considered until that very moment. *What if I <u>didn't</u> pray? What would happen? Would Mr Jesus, Mr God and Mrs Mary know? I mean . . . they are very busy people. They must be . . . because they never answered my wishes for peace or happy people. Or help with my family tree. I never got an answer about that. Maybe I won't talk to them tonight.* She felt sheepishly guilty then naughty and defiant even, but at the same time somewhat justified. Without a further thought, she decided to hop straight into bed and snuggle her teddy to sleep.

'You no pray!'

A loud thunder. The door flung open and Paupau stood gigantic over the doorway, her 5'1 frame imposing in shadow.

'What do you mean, Paupau? I did pray.'

It was the first lie she had ever told, and it was to her beloved Paupau. She couldn't believe how quickly and easily it slid out, like silky cheung-fun. As soon as the words left her mouth, she felt a hard lump in her throat. *This must be what sin feels like.*

'You no pray! You naughty girl! You lie! Bad girl. You stand up now! Stand up! Stand up now!'

Paupau's voice roared through the girl's ears as she leapt out of her bed and stood at attention, petrified. Her Paupau had never raised her voice at the girl before, and the power of her anger frightened the girl. Suddenly hot beads of tears gathered in her eyes as she began to shake.

'You kneel now in front of Mr Jesus. KNEEL!' rumbled Paupau as her granddaughter's buckling knees slammed onto the wooden floor.

The girl was too frightened to register the painful bang of floor on her knees.

'You say the truth. Now! You spoke a lie! You spoke a lie!' continued Paupau.

Her granddaughter stared up at Paupau and then the crucifix, utterly speechless. She wanted to scream out that she was sorry, that she didn't mean it, that she just wanted to see what would happen, but nothing came out.

'You know what happen to children who lie? You know? I tell you. Satan, he come from closet. Yes, this one. This closet.'

Her granddaughter's eyes sprinted to the closet. She thought of how the night-lamp created shadow play against their built-in wardrobes each night, shadows which now horrified her, shadows of demons.

'Satan,' Paupau continued. 'He come from closet, he hook your soul from inside your mouth. Take soul and drag soul down to Hell with him. Your body stay here. No soul. Like dead. Your soul stay in Hell FOREVER!'

'AHHHHHHHH!' she shrieked at the top of her lungs, stupefied at what her Paupau had told her.

Uncontrollable wailing screams and tears spewed from the girl as she repeated how sorry she was and begged her Paupau for her forgiveness.

'P . . . lease Paupau . . . ple-ase! I . . . I don't want Satan . . . I don't want . . . I-I-I am so . . . so so-rrryy. Please! No Satan. Please!'

'Okay. So now you pray every night, yes?' Paupau looked at her granddaughter with a stern face.

The girl nodded frantically, her tears and mucus clinging onto her face. She was still shaking from the threat that Satan would come hook her soul away from her.

She couldn't sleep that night nor for the next three nights. Each night she was terrorised by the shadow play created by her night-lamp, which now looked like Satan and his demons dancing towards her, waiting for her to make that one mistake before he would come and hook her soul out from her throat. On the third night, tired of being terrorised by her vivid imagination and exhausted from the lack of sleep, she got rid of the night-lamp altogether. She figured if Satan was going to come for her, she may as well get a good night's sleep beforehand. She had heard that you don't get much sleep in Hell. For the rest of her childhood, she prayed every night without fail, even if she never really understood for what or why she was praying.

To this day she sleeps in utter darkness because sometimes it's less scary when we can't see our demons.

SEVEN

LUNAR FLOWERS

Every family has their own traditions. The girl's family had traditions, customs, religious rituals and superstitions—a result of mixing staunch Roman Catholicism, Chinese ancestral worship, Buddhism (particularly reverence for Kwun Yum) and a pinch of Paupau-ism. It was a mishmash of eccentric do's and don'ts which to an outsider made absolutely no sense, but to the girl's family, everything was perfectly logical.

One superstition revolved around the blossoming of narcissus bulbs on the first day of the Lunar New Year, which her family believed not only brought prosperity to the household but also meant the Virgin Mary would bless them throughout the upcoming year. For it to be a truly double-lucky year, their family needed to ensure both good luck from the East and blessings from the West! East, West, all areas needed to be covered. This mishmash of East and West was not uncommon in many Hong Kong families who had embraced Christianity but often continued with their Chinese traditions out of reverence for their cultural heritage.

Every year since she could remember, her Paupau would take her to the wet market to methodically pick out the best 'flower roots', the bulbs from which these auspicious narcissus flowers would bloom. The roots had to be inspected for blemishes, weighed in Paupau's judging hand for substance and sniffed for potential. Observing her Paupau, she understood this was no trivial undertaking, it was a science—a Paupau science. It made the girl so proud that her Paupau would take her along for such an important task.

Every year without fail their family was blessed because every year, as if by some mystical timer, the narcissus flowers would bloom precisely on the first day of the Lunar calendar, perfuming their small flat for the next three days. Every year, as soon as Paupau saw that they were double-lucky, she would kneel in front of the racially questionable portrait of the Virgin Mary and offer her heartfelt and devout gratitude. The girl would look at her Paupau with bewildered admiration. *Paupau's prayers must be very powerful. She must really be good friends with Mr Jesus and Mrs Mary. We are very lucky to have pretty flowers to bless the home again this year. Yes, Paupau's prayers are SO great,* she would think to herself and nod along as if confirming her thoughts.

But not every year can be a double-lucky year because sometimes prayers are neither heard nor answered. Sometimes you've picked a bad batch and the bulbs aren't ready. Sometimes things just didn't work out the way her Paupau had intended. The Lunar New Year Eve finally came to pass when the bulbs had sprouted tall stems of gorgeous white narcissus buds, pregnant and ready to burst. But on the day of, they were still sealed airtight, not quite ready to sprout out into the world. *This isn't good. Not good at all.*

'Ah-ya. What to do? What to do?! No good! No good at all. Bad sign. Very bad,' Paupau exclaimed, as she slapped her hands together and raised her palms up as if to interrogate the Heavens.

'It's okay, Mother. They are just flowers. If they don't blossom today, they will blossom tomorrow,' reasoned the girl's mother.

'Ha?! They just flowers? No! They not just flowers. They give good luck. Blessing from Mrs Mary. Blessing for New Year. No flower, no blessing! No luck! No good! No good equals BAD! Ah-ya!' exclaimed Paupau as she slapped her hands together, this time even louder as if to tell off her insolent daughter.

'Hmmm. Judging by the way the buds look tonight, even if you add some fertilisers and put a lamp next to it, it doesn't look promising,' offered Auntie Yin.

'Ah-ya! This is awful. So awful. Ah-yah! What to do now? What to do?' protested Paupau, but it was too late. It was already eight p.m. and they still needed to head to the supermarket down the road to purchase some last-minute groceries.

With a heavy head, Paupau slipped on her open-toed sandals and readied her handbag. Despite the fact that it was late January and less than 15 degrees Celsius outside (cold by Hong Kong standards), Paupau always wore sandals. Rain, sun, typhoon, cold or hot—sandals. During the winter, her Paupau would add a pair of ankle-length skin-tone Lycra tights which her daughters would tease her for. 'A Hakka farmer's daughter, always a Hakka farmer's daughter!' they would laugh. Paupau would simply huff and ignore their teases.

'You want ice cream?' asked the girl's mother.

'Yes! Please! Chocolate! PLEASE!'

The girl was delighted. *Ice cream just before Lunar New Year, what a treat!* the girl thought to herself.

'I'll come too. I need to get some fruits for tomorrow,' said Auntie Yin. 'You guard the home and stay here. Remember, call 999 if there is an emergency, okay?'

Auntie Yin was always ready to award her niece any available opportunity to make her more independent and responsible.

In a flurry the three women dashed out and left the girl alone. All she could think about was how distressed her Paupau was about the narcissus. She couldn't bear the thought of her beloved Paupau being even more upset tomorrow and who knows, for the whole year! Her grandmother's words kept playing round in her head. *Bad luck year. No good! No good!* She couldn't stop fixating on the thought that her Paupau would somehow take the blame onto herself. *Ah-yah! All my fault. No good. Useless. All my fault.* Something had to be done.

The girl stood in front of the expectant buds and examined them from left to right. First, she tried clapping her hands next to them, having recalled seeing something like that in a film—flowers responding to sound, or was it a song? *Clap. Clap. Clap.* No response. Then she tried talking to them, charmingly negotiating with the buds to blossom and in exchange she would never pick the flowers off their stems ever again.

'Now flowers, I know you don't want to wake up and get moving, but if you do, I'll make a deal with all of you. I'll never pick a single flower again. I promise! Deal?'

No response. Clearly all those films and cartoons she had watched were gross exaggerations of reality. *Never mind.* She needed to bring in the big guns and take action herself.

'Well, if clapping won't work, asking nicely won't work, and prayers won't work then, flowers, you leave me no choice! My Paupau is going to get what she wants whether you like it or not!' threatened the girl.

And with that, the girl took a single bud gently in between her fingers and began to peel the petals open, prising them open with her stumpy fingers and chewed nails. As soon as she had successfully opened the first one, she gasped, 'This is going to work! Yes. It worked!'

She was on a mission for her Paupau. One by one, she prised open the narcissus buds until every single one of them had borne into the world their swollen smiles. When it was all done, the girl sat back on the black leather sofa, crossed her arms and legs with immense pride. *I did it! Now, just wait until they come home! I can't wait! They are going to be so happy. Paupau will be so happy. I have saved Lunar New Year! Maybe I'll get even more lai-see!* She was beaming with smiles, especially at the prospect of getting more lai-see—red envelopes stuffed with good luck money given to children during Lunar New Year.

She could hear the metal clangs of the gate and the door being unlocked. Giddy smiles had to be contained; she didn't want to spoil the surprise. Keeping it together, she tried her best to sit nonchalantly. Her mother and Auntie Yin sat at the dining table peeling tangerines as they chatted away whilst Paupau, still devastated about the flowers, started to mop the parquet floor. She wanted to make sure she got all her cleaning done before Lunar New Year as it was bad luck to clean on New Year's Day. As Paupau got closer to the windowsill where the flowers sat, the girl was bursting to tell her Paupau. She couldn't help it. She had to say something.

'Look, Paupau! It's a miracle! The flowers. They have all blossomed!' the girl declared.

'Ah-ya! What is this? What happened?' Paupau paused. 'Oh my! It is true! The flowers! They are all open! How is this possible? Thank you, Mr God. Thank you, Mr Jesus. Thank you, Mrs Mary. Thank you. Thank you!'

Paupau was beside herself with utter joy. Over and over she kept repeating that it was a miracle and that they were truly blessed.

'Ha? What? Really? That is amazing,' shouted the girl's mother, rushing towards the flowers to see this Lunar New Year miracle for herself.

'Oh yes, it is true. The flowers have opened! I can't believe it. How this even possible? They really open? So quickly? Well, that's really great.'

The mother was relieved that the flowers were now all open, which meant her own mother would be more manageable for the next few days.

'Wait. One. Second,' halted Auntie Yin, holding up a finger, eyes and brows narrowing. 'Not possible. This is not possible.'

'What do you mean not possible? Can't you see the flowers have blossomed? We are blessed,' Paupau assured her.

'Not possible,' said Auntie Yin whose eyes now turned to the girl and then to the flowers.

Her niece started to become very nervous. She knew Auntie Yin was on to her. Oh yes, she knew but she hoped to God that nothing further would be said. She really didn't want the happy illusion to be spoilt for her beloved Paupau. Auntie Yin inspected the flowers with great scrutiny and then her lips curled.

'Did you PEEL the flowers?' asked Auntie Yin.

'What do you mean? No,' the girl lied.

This was lie number two. The first had been about praying. *Oops*.

'I ask you again. Look at me. Did you <u>peel</u> the flowers?' interrogated Auntie Yin, this time with her mother and Paupau standing right behind her Auntie.

The girl looked up and all she could see were three grumpy frowns on three very irritated women staring back at her. She felt awful, guts all inside out and back to front. Her Auntie Yin continued to glare at the girl, waiting for her to break. And break she did. Before she knew it, her mother had grabbed yet another racially questionable picture of Jesus, shoved it in the girl's face and forced her to swear on Jesus, on the pain of Hell, that she had not peeled the flowers open.

The girl could not take it any more. She had already been so stupefied with fear of Hell, demons and Satan that she crumpled. Spewing tears and apologies, she desperately tried to explain her actions.

'I . . . I just want-ted . . . just want-ted Paupau . . . Paupau to be . . . .be . . . be happy . . . I-I-I-I . . . I didn't mean . . . .mean to. I-I-I-I. Paupau . . . ha-aa-py.' The girl was heaving, choking, snorting her words out.

The three women looked upon the girl whose ice cream lolly had melted all over her trembling hands and onto her thighs. What a chocolate mess of a child. Shaking their heads, the girl's mother began to laugh.

'What you laughing at? Not funny. Stop laughing. Nothing to laugh about,' tutted Paupau, who felt pity for the girl.

'It's funny. Isn't it? You fell for it. Even I did! We both fell for it! Ha! Only Ah-Ying was clever enough to figure it out. We are so stupid! Fooled by a nine-year-old child!' laughed the mother, who had now returned to the dining table and continued to peel her tangerines.

'Little one,' frowned Paupau. 'Very dishonest of you. You spoke lie when we asked. That was wrong. Very wrong. But I understand,' said Paupau calmly yet sternly. 'It's late. Go shower, pray and to sleep. Remember confess your sins. Lots of sins today.'

The girl nodded. Embarrassed and covered in chocolate, she decided it would be best to do as she was told.

From the bathroom she could hear the women gossiping about her. She heard words never associated with her before being spoken. Words like naughty. Mischievous. Deceitful. Lying. Cunning. Deceptive. She didn't like those words being spoken about her. They made her feel guilty—a feeling she was familiar with—but there was also a new feeling, one she had never experienced before: defiance. Something had begun to brew inside. The more she replayed those words in her head, the angrier she became, although she didn't understand why. *Naughty. Mischievous. Deceitful. Lying. Cunning. Deceptive. But that's not me . . . is it?*

That night lying in bed, in the pitch black, she couldn't sleep. All she could think about was why they had made such a big deal out of her special gardening skills. She could understand why they would be angry that she lied about it but couldn't get her head around why making flowers open for her Paupau was such a criminal offence. *If I want to open the flowers, why do I need to wait? Why do I need to wait for magic or prayers to open them? Why can't I do it myself? Why do I have to wait for Mr Jesus or Mrs Mary to open them? They are busy. And if it is to make my Paupau happy, why can't I do it? Why can't I open them myself?* So many questions.

EIGHT

DEATH LESSONS

'Paupau, what happens when I get older?' queried the girl. She was six years old at the time.

'You grow up. Become like Auntie Yin. Young university student. Bright future. Must study and work hard.'

'Paupau, what happens after that?'

'You grow older. Become like your mother. Woman with a family of her own. Many responsibilities. Have to work hard to make money. Lots of bills to pay. Look after your own mother—your duty as a daughter. Must work hard.'

'Oh. What happens after that?'

'You become old like me. You become a Paupau. Wrinkly skin, bad knees. But many grandchildren look after you and make you happy.'

'Oh. And then what happens?'

'After that you die.'

Immediately the girl burst into tears. In a single phrase, her Paupau instilled in the six-year-old girl her first lesson about life and death—that growing up meant studying hard, working even harder, to eventually meet an unavoidable death.

The girl's second death lesson was when she was eight years old. A No. 8 Signal typhoon had hit Hong Kong with a windspeed up to 100 km per hour. Bamboo frames lining half-constructed buildings trembled as the famous neon signs that cluttered Hong Kong's streets in Wan Chai and Tsim Sha Tsui swung wildly. Small trees were uprooted and blown away. Cross-harbour ferry services were cancelled, and public transport was limited. Everyone was instructed to go home, stay indoors and keep all windows closed. But this family was different; this family waited for Signal Eights to venture out.

'It's human-kite time. Let's go have some fun. Get yourself ready,' ordered her mother.

The girl quickly gobbled the last few morsels of rice as Paupau cleared the dining table, shaking her head disapprovingly.

'Not safe. You cannot take her with you. It's too dangerous. Ah-ya! She can get hurt! You are all crazy! How did I raise such insolent daughters?' scolded Paupau, but it was onto deaf ears.

'Bigger T-shirt this time for better wind-catching effect. Last time your T-shirt was too small,' said Auntie Yin as she threw one of her oversized T-shirts at the girl.

'You remember, right? To wear a swimming suit underneath, you know, just in case you fall into the sea. Don't forget towels. Put them in a plastic bag.'

The girl was giddy with nervous excitement, for she hadn't been taken to play human-kite with her mother and Auntie Yin for some time—there simply hadn't been strong enough typhoons to do so.

Bags prepared, the three walked half a block down the road to their local taxi stand and jumped into a taxi, ready for a night of exhilaration.

'Where are you going?' asked the taxi driver.

'Wan Chai Pier,' replied the mother.

'Sorry?'

'Wan Chai Pier,' she repeated.

'Eh, okay. Are you sure? Miss, it's a Signal Eight typhoon out there!'

'Yes, we are sure. Wan Chai Pier, please.'

The taxi driver was confused and looked extremely concerned at the sight of the two shabbily dressed women with a bin liner for a handbag and a mixed-race girl wearing a T-shirt big enough to be a dress asking to be taken to the pier during a Signal Eight typhoon. But a fare is still a fare, so he obliged.

When they arrived, Auntie Yin secured their bin liner to a lamppost and they scouted the area for the best angle to catch the wind.

'Can you swim?' asked her mother rhetorically.

Her mother knew the girl could swim but the question was their way for the girl to give consent. She could swim, so if she were to end up in the water, she would theoretically be fine.

'Yes. I can swim,' declared the girl with pride.

'Good. You remember how to do, yes? Stand here, hold my hands.'

Her mother led her close to the edge of the pier. Although the rain and wind were beating at the girl's face fiercely, she could still see Hong Kong's famous skyline and just about spot the Regent Hotel across the harbour.

'Okay. I let go on "fly" okay? Three-two-one, FLY!'

On that cue her mother let go as the girl spread her arms like a swallow learning to fly. The wind caught the back of her T-shirt like a sail and the girl felt herself glide across the floor. There was no better feeling. *I'm flying! I'm flying! Hahaha! I'm flying!* It was the thrill of a lifetime.

'Hey! You! What are you doing here?' shouted a man's voice. Two men who looked like policemen marched hastily towards them.

Auntie Yin quickly threw a towel over the girl to keep her warm. The girl peeked out of her hooded towel through wind-battered eyes and watched as the two policemen shouted at her mother.

'What are you doing here? And with such a small child? This is not safe!' scolded one of the men.

'We're just enjoying the pier.'

'Miss, it's a Signal Eight typhoon. It is not safe, certainly not with a young child—is she your daughter?'

The other man, who seemed to be calmer, smiled at the girl.

'Yes. Yes, she is.'

'We are here to enjoy the wind and the experience. We are not breaking any laws. This is a public area,' said Auntie Yin with her chest puffed out as if she were ready for war.

'That may be so, but it is extremely dangerous to be out here. Your daughter could be swept away into the sea and drown! We advise you to leave immediately or we will have to take you all into custody for your safety.'

The man gestured to their vehicle—they were indeed police officers, and the two women had no intention of spending their evening in a police car so decided it best to comply.

'Yes, yes. Okay. Sorry, ah-Sir. Okay. We're leaving,' assured her mother obligingly. Or at least she had pretended to leave as she sluggishly grabbed their belongings and waited for the policemen to leave. As soon as they were out of sight, it was back to playing human-kite. But the girl found it hard to continue. The threat of the policeman's words of her being swept away into the sea, drowning and dying killed her carefree attitude. She didn't want to die, definitely not today, so she decided to console herself. *But I can swim. So even if I fall in, I will swim. If I swim, I won't drown, if I won't drown, I won't die. Silly policeman! He doesn't know I can swim!*

The next morning, as expected, school was cancelled. Paupau had made the girl's favourite spicy rice noodles with braised pork and bamboo shoots and she perched in front of the TV, slurping her bowl of warm deliciousness. The girl almost choked on the spicy broth as she watched speechlessly at the havoc Typhoon Koryn had wreaked. It was shocking. Neon signs littered the streets, flipped motorbikes, broken shop windows. That wasn't all. Some unfortunate pedestrians had been swept by heavy rainfalls and mudslides and died. The policeman's alarms rang in her head. *Swept away. Drown. Die.* The girl took a big gulp of air. *Swept away. Drown. Die.*

That was the last time the girl played human-kite. She wasn't convinced her swimming skills would be enough to save herself from drowning in the Hong Kong harbour.

Her third death lesson was when she was nine years old and in the French Alps. It was the first time they had ventured to Europe and the second time the girl had experienced snow. Travelling all the way to France was a big deal back then for local families who often could not afford the costly plane fare.

Unable to ski, the girl was perfectly content with her bright red sleigh and her beginner's slope. The gorgeous glistening snow had become her new best friend as she happily trudged up and sleighed down, repeating the tiresome act of going up and down, up and down, over and over. Seeing that the girl was safe and had fine-tuned her sleighing abilities, her mother and Auntie Yin left the girl to it and went off to learn how to ski. By the time her mother had returned, the girl was exhausted but felt that climbing for the few seconds of excitement was worth it.

'Hey! How about we ride together?' said the girl's mother, standing over the girl and her red sleigh.

The girl looked over to the bigger slope— the very adult slope. It was so high and steep that it unnerved the girl. She didn't want to go down it. It was too scary. She wanted to stay within the confines of her small baby slope—it was safe and secure. But her mother insisted, grabbed the sleigh and marched them over to the top of the big slope.

'Don't worry, I'm with you,' assured her mother and planted the girl onto the sleigh in front of her.

Before the girl even had a chance to show her mother where the sleigh brakes were, her mother had pushed them off and they shot down the slope like a bullet.

'Stop! Stop! Please! STOP! It's too fast! MUMMY! STOP!' shrieked the girl at the top of her voice.

Panicked, her mother pulled at the rope in front, assuming it was for the brakes. The momentum of the pull flipped their entire sleigh over. The girl went flying and plummeted down the massive slope, rolling like a ragdoll. Her mother, heavier and stronger, was able to break her own fall as she watched her daughter continue to flop, bounce and tumble, until finally she came to a stop.

Bright red blood stained the snow around the girl. Her limbs felt twisted and sore, and her head was pounding. Petrified at the sight of bright crimson on the white snow, the girl shrieked and cried. Mucus. Tears. Blood. The whole lot. Her mother crawled up towards her and cradled the girl as she squeezed her fingers between the bridge of the girl's nose to stop it from bleeding.

'I'm so sorry. My God. I'm so sorry. I didn't know. It was my fault. I am so sorry. Please don't cry.'

Her mother's eyes looked different; they were the eyes of someone afraid. She had never seen her mother afraid before and now seeing that fear in her eyes ignited the girl's anger.

'You don't listen. You didn't listen to the instructions. You just did it. You . . . it's your fault!' screamed the girl. 'You never listen to me . . . the break was on the side. The side! THE SIDE!'

The girl had lashed out. She had never lashed out like that at her mother before, but she was exasperated at how careless her mother had been. The girl was now in a frenzy and all her mother could do was hold her daughter and rock her back and forth.

Sometimes mothers should keep certain frightening thoughts to themselves. Sometimes mothers should know what not to say to their frenzied daughters, but her mother was different and didn't understand this important parental fact. Her mother, upon spotting a massive gaping hole in the middle of the slope, thought it was appropriate to share this with her daughter.

'Oh my God! Look! That big hole!' her mother pointed to the crater. 'We are so lucky we didn't fall inside. If we fell . . . we would break so many bones, maybe even die! Oh my God! So lucky. We so lucky we didn't die.'

The girl looked up at the crater and trembled. Her vivid imagination ran wild as she pictured what it would have been like to fall through. The fear of what could have potentially happened was worse than the bitter cold that had begun to seep into her layers of clothes.

Without skis, neither the girl nor her mother was permitted on the ski lift to return them to the top. Between her mother's lack of French and the ski lift operator's piggish ignorance, there was no other option than to climb back up. The girl looked up and took a big gulp. The sight of the steep and monstrous snow slope made every part of her ache. *No choice. No other way. Got to go back up there*, she told herself as she put one foot in front of the other, fingers clawing and grasping at whatever she could. One foot in front of the other, she kept going. Her mother, who was uncharacteristically silent throughout the whole time, remained right behind the girl in case she fell or slipped off.

One foot after the other, step by step. *No choice. No other way. Got to go back up there.* Her fingers and toes were so cold she could no longer feel them. Occasionally she slipped and skidded down, but each time she kept going, even more determined to reach the top. *I am like that Greek man Mrs Morris told me about at school.* She attempted to occupy her mind by trying to recall the name of the Greek myth she had read about at school. *Sissy-fuss! His name was Sissy-fuss!* By the time she remembered, she had managed to reach the top. When she did, she fell on her knees and cried. She was so relieved that she made it and that she was alive.

'Hey, where have you been?' asked Auntie Yin, totally unaware of what had happened. 'I've been waiting for you two for hours! Why is she crying?'

'I tell you later,' replied the mother.

For months, the girl kept having a recurring nightmare that had varying details and endings. Each time it started the same way—she would be on a sleigh that suddenly lost control. Sometimes she would roll down an endless slope. Sometimes she would roll into a crater in the middle of the slope and fall in until she crashed to the bottom. Sometimes she would fall down the slope and never get to the end, just a continuous descent downwards. Other times she would never be able to reach the top of the slope, instead she would be trapped struggling uphill for ever. But in every single nightmare she was always alone. Her mother was never to be found. No one was there to help or save her. Not seeing her mother in any of her nightmares shifted something within the girl. She didn't know what it was exactly, but the seed of doubt in her mother had already been planted and it was growing.

That was the girl's third death lesson. Since that day she understood that anyone, at any point, could and would die. She was simply lucky. She hated snow ever since.

NINE

OVER 35 WAYS

'Mummy, when is Daddy coming home?'

'Not for a long time.'

'Why? Where is he?'

'He's on long business trip. Very long. In America.'

'Oh.'

'Those stamps from America you collect—they are from your father's letters.'

'Oh, I see. So, Daddy writes to me?'

'Yes. Your father writes letters to you.'

So long as the letters from her father kept coming, albeit sporadically, the girl was relatively satisfied with the notion that her father was on some big important business trip in the land of opportunity. How wonderful and proud she felt— her father in America making money. At the time she had no idea what America was except that it was where her favourite cartoon mouse Fievel and his family dreamt of going. But after some time, the holes within her mother's concocted story could no longer be covered up and the girl's inquisitive nature could no longer be appeased with 'business trip'. After all, how long can a business trip be? Months? Years?

When the letters became less frequent and finally stopped, when there were no more pretty USA stamps to collect, when her mother could no longer tell her daughter that her father was still on the same business trip that he had been on for over three years, the girl had had enough. She wanted some answers. The last time she recalled seeing her father was when she was only four years old and now that she was almost eight, she wasn't sure if her fragmented memories of her father were real or imagined.

'Is my father coming back?'

'I don't know.'

'Why?'

'Because we got a divorce.'

'What's a divorce?'

She had heard this word before in films and in whispers at school amongst her friends. She was quite certain she knew what a divorce was but wanted to hear it from her own mother's mouth. She felt she was old enough now to understand what a divorce really meant and that her father wasn't going to come home anytime soon.

'A divorce is . . . when a husband and wife no longer want to stay or be together. They don't want to be married any more. And the husband goes away,' sighed her mother.

'Is that why my father is gone? Because you got that, what, a divorce?'

'Yes. He went back to America.'

The girl paused to think. A long pause.

'Why did he stop writing to me?'

'I don't know.'

For a few years, the girl left the subject of her father's whereabouts in the corner of her psyche but by the time she was around eleven years old, that niggling itch to know more had spread throughout her entire being. She had enough of being unable to complete family trees at school or of having such a strange-sounding surname but being unable to explain why. She resented how she was often singled out for being the only 'guai' in the family and teased for her stocky frame, chubby legs, rough skin and wild frizzy hair—features she had inherited from her Western side. She was well aware she was half-white but ashamed that she was unable to explain where she was from and that shame made her angry.

One day, out of the blue, the girl decided it was time to take action, so she walked up to her mother who was sat at the dining table and said, 'Mum, I want to find my father.'

It seemed as if her mother had been preparing for this day. She had stashed records of her ex-husband's addresses in the US, an address of his mother's home, his expired passport and even his Social Security Number. Her mother figured all this would be enough to find him, or at least find someone who would be able to tell them where he was.

So, upon her daughter's request, the mother wrote a letter to her father's last known address, which was the girl's grandmother's home. She explained that they had been married and their daughter, with whom he hadn't made any contact in almost six years, was eager to hear from her father.

The girl had never met her paternal grandmother before and until that moment she had never given it much thought. But as soon as the notion of another grandmother came to light, she was thrilled. *Wow! Another grandmother! Like Paupau but American! This is so great. I've now got two grandmothers. Oh, I hope to meet her one day. This will be so great. Yes! Wow!*

But childish dreams, born of more emotion than experience, tend to get crushed, and for the girl it was no different.

LETTER 1 CIRCA 1994

I am writing this letter in response to your fax just received. I do not know who you or your daughter are. Nor have I ever heard of either of you.

I do have a son who lived in Hong Kong a long time ago. During this time we did not hear from him. We only heard from him when he returned with a problem that was straightened out years later. He did live with my husband and myself for 3 years after he returned. He now works in a country called Thailand. He keeps in touch, we hear from him once a month and he does call once every couple of months.

I cannot see good. When my son calls I will let him know you wrote a letter to contact him. It would be up to him. Did you know he has a family here in the USA? Are you sure you have the right person?

The girl's mother was reluctant to show her the letter, but the girl insisted.

'If my grandmother wrote back, I want to read what she said,' demanded the girl.

It was a very difficult letter to read. Each word felt like a slap to the face. Without prompting, her mother sat down and wrote a reply, this time enclosing the only photograph that they had of the girl's father when he was a young boy. It was a black-and-white family portrait, taken perhaps at a family picnic with her grandmother, grandfather, uncle, auntie and her father, who looked around nine or ten. She had never met any of them, they might as well have been complete strangers. But she knew, and they knew, that they were her kin.

The girl protested, not wanting her mother to enclose the photograph because she knew she would probably never get it back. But her mother decided that this was the only way they could squash all doubt that Herman, the girl's father, was whom they had been searching for.

LETTER 2 CIRCA 1994

I have received your letter and the photo and the marriage certificate that you included. I do believe you had some kind of relationship with my son but I have no idea what type of relationship it was nor what happened as neither you nor your daughter were ever mentioned.

I had forwarded your letters to my son with this letter. It is totally up to him to contact you. That is the only thing I can do for you. I cannot give you his address. He knows how to reach you.

I told you in my last letter that he lives in Thailand. I feel that we should not be in any future contact. I informed several members of my family and they are of the same opinion. I believe if my son wanted me and our family to know he would have done so. I and my husband are ill.

PLEASE NO MORE FUTURE CONTACT. Take care of yourself and your daughter.

'Do you want me to write back?' the girl's mother spoke softly whilst she tried to read the girl's face, hoping the gentle tone would ease the blow.

'No, Mum. No need. Don't write back,' she said in a calm and cold voice.

'Are you sure?'

'Yes, I am sure,' said the girl.

Slow uncertain steps dragged her towards her desk. Her knees buckled as she felt all her energy being sucked out of her. She felt like she was devoid of an endoskeleton as she sat at her desk and pulled out her thesaurus.

She had heard the word 'abandoned' before but until that moment it had never crossed her mind to associate it with herself. 'Abandoned' was a word used for infants left on church doorsteps for nuns to find—it was a word reserved for orphans, not a word for her. *Did Daddy abandon me? Did I do something wrong? Why doesn't he want me? Was I not a good girl? Why doesn't he want me? He has another family? Why does he have another family? Does he love his other family more than me? Why doesn't he want me?*

She looked up 'abandoned' and found there were over thirty-five different synonyms for it. Many of the words she had never seen before nor did she know how to pronounce them. As she read through the list, uncontrollable thoughts swarmed her mind, splicing extracts from her grandmother's letter, making her guts churn. She felt nauseous.

She looked down at the synonyms and she picked out the ones she knew and scratched them down into her notebook. The other words which she hadn't encountered before or was unsure of, she decided to leave out. She wasn't sure why, but she felt compelled to write these words down as if to document her pain. With each word etched in blue biro, she tried to formulate a sentence next to it, hoping to make some sense of how she felt.

1. *Deserted—My father deserted me and my mum.*
2. *Bailed out—He had bailed out on us.*
3. *Quit—He quit wanting to be my dad.*
4. *Renounced—He renounced being my dad.*
5. *Dumped—My father dumped me.*
6. *Ditched—My father ditched me.*
7. *Wash hands of—He washed his hands of me.*
8. *Run out on—He ran out on us.*
9. *Forsaken—I am forsaken.*
10. *Disowned—I feel disowned.*
11. *Stranded—I feel stranded by him.*
12. *Shunned—He has shunned me.*
13. *Quit—My father quit being my father.*
14. *Castaway—I am now a castaway.*
15. *Cast off—because he had cast me off.*
16. *Cast aside—he had cast me aside.*
17. *Rejected—He rejected me.*
18. *Neglected—He neglected me.*
19. *Forgotten—I am a forgotten daughter.*
20. *Alienated—I have been alienated from him.*
21. *Resigned—He resigned from being my dad.*

22. Discarded—He discarded me like I meant nothing.

23. Unwanted—I am unwanted.

The list went on. There was a small part of her that had hoped that by attributing language to her pain she could somehow process her grief. But it didn't work. Instead, every synonym and its accompanying sentence brought her closer to facing up to the harsh reality that her father wasn't coming back, ever.

Up until that day, the girl had lived in a state of suspended disbelief—a kind of limbo fantasy. Although she didn't know when or if she would see her father again, this continued state of uncertainty maintained a small flicker of hope within her. But in a single letter, what little childish hopes the girl had were extinguished.

The girl would come to learn over the years that her father was never coming back and had indeed abandoned her. She would also come to realise that there are far fewer words for 'abandoned' in Cantonese than there are in English and that her Hong Kongese side of the family had never abandoned her. But what she could not grasp, even to this day, was why he had decided not to tell any of his family about his daughter's existence.

He didn't even tell her. He didn't tell her I existed. Do I? Why? Why didn't he tell her? She's my grandmother . . . she's my family and she doesn't even want to know about me. Why didn't he tell her?

She didn't matter enough to her father for him to tell anyone she existed. She didn't matter enough. Which seemed to her to be the equivalent of not existing at all.

PAUPAU LOGIC

'When you cry, you must pick up tears. No crying. Must pick up tears. Crying cannot help feed you.'

'No wear slippers, you get wide feet. Wide feet same as ugly feet. Ugly feet is no husband. No man wants wife with wide feet. Put your slippers on.'

'Must learn to cook. Cannot cook means cannot keep husband. Happy husband stomach happy marriage.'

'Eat noodles on birthday. Long noodles long life.'

'Anything number four no good. Stay away from number four. Bad luck.'

'When sunshine, carry umbrella. Don't get so dark. Dark skin means to work outside. Means poor. No man wants marry a dark skin wide feet girl.'

'If bruise, boil egg. Must hard boiled. Peel shell off quickly. Wrap it in a cloth and put it on the bruise. Bruise disappear.'

'Don't eat oranges when have cough. Make cough more.

Tiger balm cure everything. Cough. Swallow tiger balm. Mosquito bite. Rub tiger balm on bite. Tummy ache. Swallow tiger balm. Aching joints. Rub tiger balm on it. Tiger balm cure everything.'

'When you have fever no eat chicken. It makes you more sick. Too much heat. Too much fat. No good.'

'Add chicken powder to cooking. Food taste better. Good food make people happy.'

'No eat fruits, dry up like old prune. No one marry you.'

'Cannot be left-handed. Not right. Must be right-handed. You're a girl. You must be right-handed.'

'Rice bucket cannot be empty. Must be full. Always full. Always with rice.'

'Don't be like me. Gong-Gong, your grandfather, beat me up. Must fight back. Must be stronger.'

'Rice, gold and salty fish. That's all you'll need to be happy.'

TEN

BUTTER FOR LAUNDRY

'Paupau, if we have a washing machine, why do you still wash my school uniform by hand? You don't need to wash by hand.'

'Ah-yah, washing machine not clean. Wash by hand, my hand, most clean.'

'But we have a machine for washing. Mummy says you don't need to wash by hand. Just put the clothes in the machine. Is it because you don't know how to use it? I can show you!'

'I know how! Of course I know. Machine uses too much water. Waste. Cannot waste water! Machine makes you soft. You young people don't know how to do anything for yourself.'

'But Paupau . . .'

'No. Come, hang laundry and I tell you funny story about laundry. Funny story from long time ago.'

* * *

We were so poor. Very poor. I tell you how poor you won't believe me. Home was a metal shack. Yes, metal. The metal sheets you see where Uncle works? Metal sheets put together by wire and wood to make a small hut. Cook, sleep, shower, toilet—all in same place. You see this living room? The hut was smaller than this. We lived like packed salty fish.

In summertime it was so hot. Very hot. Heat and humidity kept locked inside, you could steam turnip inside it was so hot. The heat made everything swell and stink. So stinky—like that smell when we go to the wet market together, you know which smell I mean? Worse than that! In wintertime it was so cold, so cold that it sunk into your bones. The metal walls were too thin, cannot keep us warm. Every time windy or raining, the hut shake, and water snuck in. No matter how many blankets we put on ourselves, we were still cold. Can't be helped, our blankets humid and damp. We go outside, it was cold. We go inside, it was cold. Inside, outside no difference. Still cold.

We lived in Tai Po, in a shanty town. Moved there with your grandfather from Tung Ping Chau Island. Ay-yah, at that time Tai Po hillside covered in squatter settlements. Clusters of metal tin huts overlapping each other. Many poor families, boat settlers, refugees. This place for people too poor to be in real home.

I already had many children by then: your big Auntie, second Auntie, your Mother, Auntie Ming, Auntie Chen and your Uncle. Auntie Yin not born yet. Many children mean many mouths to feed. Not enough money and many mouths to feed means poor. Poor means hunger. Ay-yah. Those were hard years.

Poor means hard work. No better motivation to work hard than empty stomach. I worked hard as a coolie carrying bricks, mortar and tools for workers who built Hong Kong. Yes! I was a coolie. I carried many catty-loads of cement and bricks. One catty around one and half pound. Up and down. All day long. I had to work very hard for little money. That little money, your grandfather—your Gong-Gong would beat it out of me when I got home so he can buy alcohol. He was a drunk. The shanty town drunk. Everyone called him Drunken Cat Man. Terrible nickname. So much shame, so terrible. Ay-ya! Everyone in the village called him that but what's worse was your mother, her brother and sisters—all called Drunken Cat Children. So shameful, how can hold head up high? Cannot. No dignity, no face. Bad enough we were so poor—the poorest in the village, even worse to be called Drunken Cat Children. All the village children poked fun at your mother and siblings, always teasing them for their father's behaviour. But what could I do? What could be done?

I hid all my money in my pockets and sewed them into my undergarments. But it didn't stop your Gong-Gong. He beat me until he found it. No matter how many cries to stop, no matter how many bruises, no matter how much blood, he didn't stop until he got his money. My life was so unfortunate. But thankfully for Mr Jesus and Mr Father Priest. If not for them, I will not be here, your mother won't be here, you won't be here either.

Mr Father Priest came to our shanty village. He handed out bags of rice and clothes to the whole village. Many people line up to get food and clothes. Mr Father Priest, he came with his group of women monks called nuns and handed out goods to us. Then he said, 'This is from Jesus.'

I asked myself, who is this Mr Jesus? This Mr Jesus is very generous, must be very rich and very powerful if he can send a Cantonese speaking guailow to come help us. Good idea to find out about this Mr Jesus—see who this man is, maybe can help us more.

So I did and in time I was baptised and became follower of Mr Jesus and Mrs Mary. Go to church every Sunday, bring all the children to learn about this important guailow who came to help us. Mr Jesus—he saved us, all of us. Mr Jesus give me something very important, something I never had before—hope. I had hope and this hope give me strength to pray this life will get better. And if not, it's okay, next life will be better! Cannot get worse!

The church people, Mr Father Priest and lady nuns—they also gave me something just as important. They gave me money, clothing and food. Altogether this make all the difference, make those years more tolerable. Otherwise, ay-yah, cannot bear.

Even though long walk, almost one hour to go to church, one hour to come back, I took your Mother, Aunties and Uncle. Go to church to pray to Mr Jesus, give him most honourable thanks and praise for sending Mr Father Priest. No one else helped us. Only Mr Father Priest and the Church. He took pity on us—he saw me with swollen lips and bruised eyes, one child in one arm, one child on back, another child in other arm. Surrounded by so many dependants. He saw your Mother and Aunties with bruises on timid tanned faces and bony thighs. They were beaten so badly by your Gong-Gong. Poor things, but your Uncle had no bruises. He was a boy, so he was spared from beatings. Your Gong-Gong never hit him, not once! Boys are more precious than treasure, so cannot hit. But girls can hit, girls worth nothing—can hit, beat, throw around. Girls no value.

Mr Father Priest, he saw, he understood and he took pity on us. After Mass each week he try to help. He offer us some money, sometimes second-hand clothes. Clothes never fit but doesn't matter, still better than nothing. Sometimes some food to fill hollow belly.

Ah-yah. Mr Father Priest, he was too good to us. Without his help, we may not survive. All those good deeds must repay, cannot not repay. That's why every week I go to church. Rain, sun, typhoon—doesn't matter, must still go to church and give thanks. Must repay. Mr God—He sees and He remembers everything, doesn't forget. Mr God has very good memory. I cannot let Mr God down. Must give thanks, must repay.

One Sunday after Mass, I recall it was wintertime, Mr Father Priest called me over to collect church donations. He gave me a solid rectangular block. Small, not very big. It was wrapped in paper with fancy squiggly guailow writing on it. Look so fancy!

I was very grateful to Mr Father Priest but both curious and a little offended that he had handed me soap. Why did he give us soap? Did we smell? Did he think we were dirty? Poor not always mean dirty. How embarrassing! We were very poor but always go to church clean. I didn't know what to say to Mr Father Priest, just thank you.

Anyhow, it was fancy soap—you know how I knew? Guailow writing. Chinese writing means local stuff. Guailow writing means Western stuff. Must be good stuff, local stuff not so good. So, we had fancy soap which must be saved for fancy clothing.

I decided to rush home. Must make clothes smell fresh and nice for church so Mr Father Priest won't think we are a dirty, smelly family. I collected all of our Sunday church clothes and filled the bath bucket with boiling water. No hot water tap like what we have today. In before time, you can't just turn on tap and by magic you have hot water. No. No magic tap. Magic taps make people soft—that's why you young kids are so soft. Everything so easy, so fast, everything can have now, everything like magic. No, we had to fetch water from the well, keep water in small rusty tank at home. One well for whole village of around fifty families. Sometimes very long line of people, sometimes even no water. No water equals no water to drink, to cook, to wash, to clean. No water means no nothing. That's why I always scold you for wasting water. No water, you die.

After collecting water, you had to carry the buckets back home without spilling. If you trip and fall, all the water spill out, you had to go back and redo all over again. When your Mother was little, she spent all day trying to collect water. After several spills, falls and trips, she learnt not to be so clumsy. She learnt—she is a fast learner, your mother. That's why she is so successful, can send you to fancy guailow private school and pay for fancy ballet lessons.

Anyhow, when you collect water you had to boil it. Like I said, no magic tap. To make the water less hot, you need to mix with cold water. Put water in large plastic tub—we call this bathtub and put all the clothing inside. Everything washed by hand and soap. No magic machine to do it for you, cannot just put in machine and press switch button. No. You had to do with own hands. Sometimes if water too hot, it scalded your skin raw and red. So painful. Sometimes water too cold, clothes not so clean. Had to get it just right.

So, I did my usual routine but this time, I had the fancy guailow soap. I was so excited to try it. Soap in one hand, clothes in other, I started scrubbing and rubbing. Rubbing and scrubbing. But why is it so greasy? Why is it getting greasier? What is this? The more I scrub with fancy soap, the greasier the clothes! And the smell! The terrible smell. Smell like lamb, smell like guailow—they have special scent—like lamb. I couldn't believe it! I didn't know what to do. How can Mr Father Priest give me such a terrible soap! If the guailows are washing their clothes with this, it is no wonder they smell like lamb! Ah-ya! I was very displeased. I emptied whole bucket and set the greasy clothes aside. I had to wash the clothes all over again, this time with cheap local soap. Three times I had to wash to get the stench out. So much water wasted. Terrible! My hands were raw when I had finished.

Next Sunday at church, I waited for all the people to leave and then to ask Mr Father Priest about the soap. I was too embarrassed. How can you question someone's good deed? It was a gift, cannot question gift. But I couldn't say nothing, cannot leave him to continue to wash his clothes with bad soap. He had no wife or mother to care for him—someone had to care for him. So, I said to Mr Father Priest, 'Mr Father Priest. Thank you for the soap last week but that soap . . . that soap you gave me, I washed and washed and washed with it, but it made my clothing so greasy and smelly that I am sorry I cannot use it. I also think you shouldn't use it either. I don't think it is good for washing. Better not to use.'

He looked at me so confused, so baffled. His big round eyes staring at me and he said, 'Soap? What soap? My dear, I didn't give you soap . . .'

I looked at him and I told him straight. I said to him, 'Yes, you did. It was wrapped in a paper with guailow writing. The soap was rectangular shape, yellow. When you gave it to me it was still hard . . . then became soft.'

You know what he say to me next? He said to me, 'OH MY DEAR!' Mr Father Priest he shouted! I never heard him shout before. But he shouted, can you believe it? A priest shouting! He shouted and shook his head, then he said, 'My dear, it was not soap! It was butter!'

'BUTTER! BUTTER!' I was shouting too! He laughed. I was red with so much embarrassment. I had never been more embarrassed nor humiliated. He must think I am just some stupid uneducated poor Hakka woman. Ay-yah. So stupid. And he continued laughing! I had never seen him laugh so much; it was very funny. He looked like white version of laughing Buddha. Seeing Mr Father Priest laugh like that, I couldn't help but laugh too.

Butter! I washed the clothes with butter! Butter for laundry! Can you believe it?

ELEVEN

SUBVERT THE GRETEL OUT

Cultural and family expectations of how a girl ought to look and behave were thrusted upon her from an early age. The girl enjoyed losing whole Sunday afternoons playing make-believe in meringue-white gowns, sparkly shoes and plastic tiaras. But as the girl grew a little older, she realised that her make-believe afternoons were a chance for her to create a world in which she could be anything she wanted. The only limit was her imagination; and so, she became her version of the ultimate princess—a princess with plastic samurai swords strapped to her back, plastic hand grenades in her pink silk handbag and a rubber AK-47 across her chest. In her mind she looked stunning.

'Ah-yah. What is this?' tutted her Paupau. 'Girls no play with swords! No! No! No! Girls no play with guns! Ah-yah! You cannot wear such beautiful dress and play with those things.'

Her Paupau shook her head and made an attempt to pry the AK-47 replica from the girl's hands.

'But Paupau, I like these toys. Look, I have many other toys too.'

The girl knelt down as she proudly laid out her trinkets from her pink silk handbag on the floor.

'See, I have my favourite My Little Pony, my makeup case. That's real lipstick you know! My grenade, a ninja star and my sparkly wand. Look, it's pink! These are all my favourites.' The girl smiled.

'Ah-yah,' sighed her Paupau again. 'Girls no play with these things. You are a girl. You must learn to play like a girl. So rough. Cannot be so rough. No one will marry you!'

'But Paupau, I'm only nine!' she chortled at how silly her Paupau sounded.

Without even realising, the girl had begun to subvert those cultural expectations of her. Expectations projected onto her from her Paupau's traditional Chinese upbringing and her mother's big hopes for her daughter. What the girl also didn't realise was that her ballet school had cultural expectations too, particularly of what a pretty ballerina girl ought to look like.

That spring, when the girl was nine years old, her ballet school announced they were putting on a professional production of *Hansel and Gretel* for their annual summer performance at the Hong Kong Cultural Centre. Auditions for Gretel were open to any female student below the age of twelve. The girl was thrilled—finally an opportunity to star in a professional ballet production! She was very confident that she'd have a shot at the lead role. *I'm going to be a real ballerina!*

'You are a good girl, my dear. A very dedicated and hardworking student. You've got lots of passion. Real passion. But for Gretel, well . . . we need someone much more delicate, much more like a <u>real</u> ballerina. I'm afraid you're too thick around the waist. Too heavy. You've got so much passion in you . . . but we need someone with daintier features and movements,' said Mrs Chan, the school's Deputy Principal, who had led the auditions and was the most appropriate person to break the disappointing news to the girl. Mrs Chan had been the girl's ballet teacher since her first class when she was only three years old.

'I'm sorry, dear.'

The girl said nothing. She was in shock, for it had never occurred to her that she wasn't 'dainty' enough or that she was 'too thick', but to them, she was simply too chunky. It was cute when she was six or seven—the chubby mixed-race girl with the stocky legs in the immaculate uniform, jumping up and down with her baby-fat belly. At nine, it had become uncomfortable for them to watch.

The other girls in her class were all Hong Kongese and had already started dieting. In the changing rooms before the lesson, they bragged to each other about how their ribs stuck out and how narrow their waists were. They wore their bony frames with pride. The girl didn't understand what there was to brag about. Her peers looked like skeletons covered in pasty translucent skin. Besides, she enjoyed food too much and the whole concept of dieting was totally alien to her. The girl was completely healthy and strong for her age, but her chunky Western frame was incompatible with the Hong Kong ideals of what a pretty ballerina ought to look like.

By the time the girl reached home, her initial befuddlement had simmered into anger. She may not have been the best ballet dancer with the sharpest techniques, but she had been pouring her heart and soul into her lessons. For every examination she was awarded distinction and often personally requested by her Principal to attend external events because she was a cute mixed-race girl.

There was nothing more she loved in this world than to dance (and to eat) but their rejection turned her to defiance. The girl decided that if she couldn't be Gretel and if she couldn't look like a dainty ballerina, then there was no point in looking like a girl anyway.

On the Sunday after her failed audition, she urged her mother to take her to the hair salon. Her mother had assumed the girl had just wanted a little trim. The girl's hair had grown to just above her waist, so her mother was not prepared for what was about to happen.

'Okay, so what are getting done today?' asked the hairdresser.

'She wants a haircut,' replied the mother.

'Sure, how short do you want it? A bob, perhaps? That would look very cute on such a pretty face,' said the hairdresser as she teased out the girl's hair.

'No,' the girl said with clenched teeth. 'Cut it off, all of it,' she instructed the hairdresser.

'Like a bob?' asked the hairdresser again, puzzled that the girl would want to chop off all that lustrous hair.

'No, like a boy. Cut it off, please,' replied the girl.

'Are you sure? But that's very short!' said the hairdresser as he looked over his shoulder for the mother's approval.

'That's too short! Are you sure? This is what you want?' added the mother.

'Yes. I am sure. Cut it all off. Like a boy,' instructed the girl unflinchingly.

She looked straight into the hairdresser's eyes through the mirror's reflection. *If I can't be Gretel, then I don't want to be a girl any more.*

'Okay, if you're sure.'

And so, her waistline-length dark brown hair was chopped off, cut short like a boy as she requested. As she studied her transformation in the mirror, she thought back to the many times her hair was used as <u>the</u> example for other students. Her hair was always referenced as what perfect ballerina hair should look like—pulled back tightly, netted, pinned, all strands glued with hair spray and gel.

'Look, this is what correct ballerina hair looks like and this is what I expect all of you to achieve. Faultless, tidy hair. Not a strand out of place. Excellent. Perfect,' showed off Deputy Principal Mrs Chan.

But that was before. Now, her hair lay lifeless on the black lacquered floor. She stared down at it—the only piece of perfect she had ever had. *If I can't be Gretel, then I don't want my hair.* She looked up at herself in the mirror and in that moment, she decided that if she could not fit into what they had expected her to look like, she would rather reject their expectations altogether.

She was on a mission. As soon as she got home, she tossed every part of her princess-archetype get-up into a large plastic bag. All the dresses, lace, sparkly shoes, threads of pearls, her silk handbag—everything. She would never play princess again.

When her ballet classmates and her teachers saw the girl's boyish haircut they gasped. It was such a rebelliously brave act, for most girls wouldn't even dream of cutting their hair that short. But things have an odd way of working out.

'My dear, your hair is so short! You look just like a boy!' exclaimed Mrs Chan.

There was a long pause. 'I have a fantastic idea. As you look just like a boy, why don't you play the role of Hansel? Hmm?'

The girl tried to contain her excitement, eyes wide open, lips bursting with glee. Without a second thought she jumped up and down shouting. *I'm going to be in the performance. I'm going to be Hansel!*

The girl would come to learn many years later that she would often be presented with two choices—to submit to cultural expectations of what a girl or woman should look and act like, or to completely forgo her version of femininity and play a male role. She had decided at nine years old on the latter.

TWELVE

DURIANS

Most children at some point would witness their mothers get annoyed, angry, emotional and even cry. Some children may even witness their mother break down in tears when life flings too much shit at them all at once and it is simply overwhelming. The girl, however, rarely saw her mother display the stereotypical 'mummy emotions' of being upset or emotional.

When the girl quizzed her mother as to whether or not she cried, her mother would just reply, 'I don't know how to. Your Paupau, whenever I cried, she would say "Pick that tear up! Not allowed! No crying!" So, I don't know how to cry.'

One day when the girl was eleven, as her mother and her were about to leave their local supermarket, her mother suddenly stopped by the exit. Something had caught her eye, something that immediately made her pupils dilate and nostrils flare.

'Here, take this,' the mother said as she handed the girl their plastic shopping bags. 'You stay still. No move. Stay here.'

Hands grasping at the bags, the girl obeyed and watched her mother storm into the pharmacy section of the supermarket.

From where she stood, the girl couldn't quite make out the words exchanged between her mother and the other woman. This woman was a whale; almost a head taller than her mother and at least twice in body mass. The girl recognised her; it was her mother's ex-tenant. The girl didn't know the full story except that this woman had taken advantage of her mother's naïve kindness and caused her a lot of financial problems.

The girl watched as her mother lost the plot at Mrs Whale. Their confrontation quickly exploded into loud shouts of profanities—combinations of words she never thought possible. Then suddenly SLAP! Mrs Whale landed a heavy hand across her mother's face. *Mum!* The girl had to restrain herself from sprinting towards her mother. *She told you to stay here. You must stay here, or you'll get in trouble.*

'Are you fucking crazy? You fat stinky cunt!' screamed her mother as she lunged at Mrs Whale.

A barrage of hammer fists, punches, pulls, grabs. Pushing, pulling. Mrs Whale grabbed her mother by the hair as the fight spilled into the rows of shopping trolleys. The security guard stood there dumbfounded as both women threw their fists at each other. Mrs Whale clutched violently at her mother's hair and refused to let go.

'Let go, you fat fucking cunt! Let go! Let go of my hair!' her mother spat out, but Mrs Whale wasn't budging as she tackled her mother up against a large display of durians.

'I said, let go!' screamed her mother. Then her mother picked up a durian from behind her and slammed it across Mrs Whale's head. WHAM! Mrs Whale fell onto the floor, screeching in horror as she realised the sharp durian spikes had left bloody scratches across her face and head.

'Oh my God! I'm bleeding! Oh my God!' Mrs Whale shrieked. 'My face! My face! You're crazy!'

As if on cue, a couple of policemen barged through the small crowd that had gathered around them and swarmed the girl's mother.

'Mum. You okay?'

The girl approached her mother, who was checking herself for wounds. A few scratches across the forearms and back, some hair ripped out, but she was completely fine.

'Madam. Please come with us,' said the police officer. The fifty-year-old-plus security guard couldn't handle the two women and had called the police. 'We need to take some statements down as to what happened. We will tend to your injuries.'

'And my daughter? Can she come with me?'

'Yes. She may come but must wait outside when you give a statement.'

The girl was so frightened for her mother as she watched them escort her to a room at the back of the supermarket whilst the girl waited alone outside. It felt like hours. *Will my mum get arrested? Is she going to jail? Am I going to lose my mum? What's going to happen?*

Just over an hour later, her mother stepped out. Her forearms were all bandaged up, which made the injuries look worse than they actually were. The girl's heart tugged—it was the first time she had ever seen her mother injured. It was a very bizarre and unnerving sight. To the girl, her mother was immortal, and now it occurred to her that she could get hurt, could bleed and could even die. It was a notion she had never had to face so directly before; it was unnerving.

'Pick up the shopping. Time to go.'

'Okay, Mum.'

'Are you okay?'

'Yes, Mum.'

'Ice cream?'

'Okay.'

Luckily the CCTV footage and witness statements matched up to her mother's statement—that it was Mrs Whale who had struck first and her mother was acting in self-defence.

'Remember, if someone hits you, you must hit them back,' instructed the mother.

'But Mr Jesus said to turn the other cheek.'

'Jesus is wrong,' spat the mother. 'Someone hits you, hit them back. Keep turning other cheek, sooner or later no more cheek to give. Must fight back, cannot be victim.'

That perhaps was one of the most important lessons the mother ever gave the girl—that irrespective of size, you must stand up for yourself, that you cannot play the victim and that you must always fight back.

MOTHER'S LOGIC

'You look very nervous. Are you nervous?'

'Yes, Mummy.'

'It's just piano exam. No need to be nervous.'

'Yes, Mummy.'

'You still look nervous. Are you nervous?'

'Yes, Mummy.'

'Drink this.'

'What is it?'

'Sherry. Help you less nervous. Play piano smoother.'

'Yes, Mummy.'

'Now you stink of alcohol.'

'Yes, Mummy.'

'Spray this.'

'What is it?'

'Perfume.'

'Yes, Mummy.'

* * *

'Mummy, mosquito bite so itchy.'

'Stop scratching and come here.'

'What's that?'

'Cigarette. Don't move.'

'Ouch!'

'See! Cigarette light burn only. Now no more itching.'

* * *

'I'm going to the cinema with some friends.'

'What friends?'

'The usual girls, and a couple of boys from school.'

'No.'

'What do you mean no? Why no?'

'You're not allowed to go out with boys.'

'But it's a big group of us.'

'No. No boys. Boys no allowed.'

'But I'm thirteen.'

'I don't care how old you are. No boys.'

'But why? I don't get it.'

'Nothing to get. No get. No boys.'

* * *

'Mum, I've got hairy legs.'

'You're half guai. Your father white man, you white too.'

'Yes, so I've got hairy legs. Hairy armpits too.'

'You're half guai. You're going to be hairy. Your father was hairy.'

'I need to get rid of it. It's gross, I need a razor.'

'No shaving. No shaving legs, no shaving underarms.'

72

'Why? I'm hairy. It's disgusting.'

'Hairless legs, hairless underarms, too much sexy-looking. Soon having sex.'

'What?! Eww. Yuck. No. I just don't want to be hairy. All the other girls shave.'

'No shaving. No hairless. If you're hairy, no sex.'

* * *

'I stink.'

'You're half guai. Your father white man, you white too.'

'Yes, but I stink. I really stink.'

'You're half guai, so you're going to stink. Your father stank.'

'I need some deodorant.'

'What? What deodorant? No deodorant.'

'Why not? I stink. Everyone else at school has deodorant.'

'So what?'

'No one is going to want to sit with me at school because I stink.'

'Then no one sits with you. Better for concentration in class.'

* * *

'Mum, I think I just got my period.'

'Really? How you know?'

'There's blood on my panties.'

'Oh. Okay. Go to Auntie Yin. She will explain.'

'But, aren't you going to . . .?'

'To do what? No. You go to Auntie Yin. She younger, she nurse. She explain.'

'But you're my mum . . .?'

'Auntie Yin nurse. She more qualified to explain.'

* * *

'What is this? Turn this off.'

'It's *American Pie*. It's funny.'

'Too much sexy. Not suitable for you.'

'What? It's a fifteen.'

'You only fourteen, not allowed.'

'But you let me watch *The Exorcist* when I was six!'

'That scary film. This sexy film.'

'And *Interview with the Vampire*.'

'That scary film too. This sexy film.'

'And what about all those Freddy Krueger films?'

'Those comedies! They made you laugh. This sexy film. Switch off now.'

'How is it a sex film? It's about teenagers. I'm a teenager.'

'It's about American teenagers. You're not American teenager. You Hong Kongese. Switch off now.'

THIRTEEN

DOMINIC

She had always wanted an older brother. Someone who would teach her how to be cool, someone who would teach her what music bands to be into, how to smoke a cigarette, how to do shots and swear like an adult. She had always wanted an older brother and, for two years, she had one in Dominic.

Dominic. Dominic was like her—half Hong Kongese and half white. And just like her parents, Dominic's parents were also divorced. He had lived with his mother in a block of flats similar to hers nearby. And just like her, Dominic didn't quite fit into either world. They were not Hong Kongese enough to be spared the 'guai' term but not quite Western enough to avoid raised eyebrows from their Western classmates at their odd food preferences. But somehow Dominic managed to take it all in stride, perhaps because, four years her senior, he had more experience and thus confidence in being of both worlds and neither world simultaneously.

To the girl Dominic was the epitome of cool; to Dominic she was the abnormally confident eleven-year-old who told him to fuck off on her first day of school. He had tried to dictate where she could and couldn't sit on the school bus on the way home.

'Excuse me. Argh, are you lost, little girl?'

Dominic towered over her. She looked up, her hair sticking to her now translucent school uniform, damp from having to change so quickly after a double P.E. swimming lesson.

'No, are you?' she replied.

Baffled, Dominic looked around to his peers as if to ask if he had heard correctly. They leaned forward in quiet astonishment, waiting to see what would unfold.

'Okay, little girl, since it's clearly your first day at school, I'm going to be nice and tell you. You wouldn't know this as you're in Year Seven. But Year Sevens sit at the front of the bus, sixth-formers sit at the back. You don't get to sit here, so just move back to where the other dorks sit.'

He was almost laughing—a sixth-former having to explain to a newbie how things worked.

'Oh, really? And who made you the dictator of the school bus?' she said, staring up at him unflinching. She had learnt from watching her mother take on Mrs Whale that she must always stick up for herself. 'And judging by that hairstyle and the homeless-person clothing, I'd say no one. Besides there aren't any more seats up there so I have to sit here. It's not like I actually want to. So, you can either shut up and sit down or you can fuck off because I'm not moving.'

The words sprinted out of her mouth before she could even think. When the last word was spoken, her face scrunched up as if to wait for a punch or slap. *This is it. You're going to die on this bus on the first day of school.*

Dead silence. The others around Dominic exchanged glances, some let out a gasp, others with eyes wide open, but none dared to whisper a single word as they all waited for Dominic's reaction.

Loud bawling laugher thundered out of Dominic's mouth.

'Ha! You've got some balls, girl! I can't believe it! I like you! You're sitting here from now on. Right next to me. Now move over,' he said as he planted himself next to her. 'I'm Dominic, by the way.'

With that she scooched over as Dominic bombarded her with questions all the way home.

From that day onwards, the girl sat next to Dominic on the school bus to and from school every day for the next two years. It was during the forty-minute bus ride each way that the girl and Dominic established their friendship, one that became fundamental to the girl's understanding of smoking, drinking, drugs, music, boys and sex. Dominic taught her more about growing up than anyone else could in less than two hours a day.

'What the fuck happened to you?' he asked as soon as she sat down.

The girl had pressed her face against the bus window, trying to conceal her face from him. It was a face of streaming tears, leaving sad marks on the glass. He pulled her shoulder back and he saw her, probably the only boy who had ever seen her cry. The girl said nothing.

'Hey, what happened? Why are you crying?' he asked, tugging at her shoulder as she tried to hide away her embarrassment.

Reluctantly she blurted it all out in tears, saliva and snot. She told him how Ranj, a boy in her year, had dumped her when she had refused to let him finger her at a friend's party over the weekend. How he called her 'frigid' and then told all his rugby friends about it and how they all took the piss out of her in the school hallways and the canteen. How they poked fun at her tomboy looks and called her a slag and trash. Everyone around could hear it.

'I don't understand, Dominic. How can I be called a slag and a frigid at the same time? It makes no sense! They contradict each other! Now everyone in my year knows about it!' she sobbed.

'Those fucking cunts. This Ranj, who's he? What year's he in?'

'He's in my Year, Year Eight. He's Suzie's brother.'

'Suzie? You mean my mate, Suzie?'

She nodded. She didn't want her pubescent problems to cause him trouble. Suzie was one of Dominic's closest friends and she didn't want things to get awkward.

'Don't worry about it. Suzie'd understand.'

The girl nodded and blew her nose. She couldn't comprehend how a handful of twelve-year-old boys could so easily eradicate her entire sense of self-worth and reduce her to a bumbling idiot clutching at tissues on a school bus. It would be a lesson she would have to learn time and time again, but for now, Dominic would take care of it for her.

The next day Dominic instructed the girl to meet him at lunch by the lower playground. She wasn't sure why, as the lower playground was where most of the sixth-formers played football and the rugby jocks gathered. It wasn't a place for someone like her; nonetheless she obliged.

As soon as the bell went, she dashed down the stairs to meet Dominic. She had been waiting for over ten minutes. Not only was she salivating from the smells enticing her from the canteen, she began to feel foolish standing there alone, staring at a gathering of sweaty popular boys. Ready to give up and leave, she spotted Dominic marching across to where Ranj sat with his posse, pulling him up by his shirt collar and dragging Ranj by the neck across the playground. Everyone stopped and stared as Dominic hauled him over to the girl.

'What have you got to say to her?'

'What? What you talking about?'

'That's your answer?' SLAP! Right to the back of Ranj's head. 'I ask again, what have you got to say to her?'

'I'm sorry?'

Ranj was both scared and confused. The girl relished every second of this exchange.

'Sorry for what?' Dominic pushed him again.

'I'm sorry for . . .? Um, sorry for dumping her?'

'You're not apologising to me, fucking idiot. Apologise to her. Own up to what you did, or I will smash your head in. Either that or I tell your sister Suzie what you did, and she can smash your head in for me.'

'Okay! Okay! I'm sorry. I'm sorry I dumped you . . . that I called you all those names.'

They were hollow sorrys but they were more than the girl ever expected to get from a boy like Ranj.

'And?'

'And I'm sorry I told my friends about you.'

'You're going to go back there to your mates, and you're going to retract and rectify everything you've said. Got it?'

Dominic pulled at his shirt collar again. A man towering over a boy. Dominic wasn't the tallest of teens but to a twelve-year-old boy, he might as well have been a giant.

The girl stood there speechless as she looked around and saw that everyone who was anyone had witnessed how one of the most popular sixth-formers in school stood up for an unknown, clumsy Year Eight tomboy. In that fantastic moment, Dominic became her male hero. She had never had a male hero before; all her childhood heroes were women, but there he was, Dominic—the older brother she had always wanted, standing up for her.

FOURTEEN

INCOMPETENT

'Your school fees are too expensive. Too high. Your teachers not teaching you correct. Too much creative. Too much drawing this, colour that, painting this. No good. Not correct way. No discipline. Not like Chinese way—memory, repetition and hard work. And your math skills—so terrible. So bad. Not learning in school. What I pay for?'

Towards the end of her first term in Year Eight, the girl's mother sat her daughter down one evening after dinner and announced to the girl that she would no longer be attending her current British-style international secondary school. Instead the girl would have to do whatever it took to get into one of the top all-girls Catholic state schools in Hong Kong. There were only two options acceptable to her mother. Option one: St. Paul's Convent School for Girls or option two: Marymount School for Girls. Option 3 did not exist. There was no option three.

The exact motive behind her mother's sudden decision was unclear. Although the mother protested that it was her school's eye-wateringly expensive fees, the girl suspected it may also have been her mother's lack of trust in the school's 'soft' way of teaching. Perhaps it may also have been her mother's view that if the girl was thrown into a submissive, hardworking, all-female environment, it would somehow mould the girl into a perfect daughter. The girl also wondered if it was because her mother had begun to sense she was leading a double life— her life at home and her life outside.

In Hong Kong culture, at home in front of parents and family members you must play the part of a dutiful and obedient child, whether you were one or not. There was no room in that culture for diversion from the norm. There were expectations about one's behaviour, appearance, speech and grades, and because of those expectations, it was a role many children learn to play flawlessly, including the girl. The girl loved her family and thus did her best to behave impeccably. She said 'please' and 'thank you', always gave or accepted things with both hands, called women and men she didn't know 'Auntie' or 'Uncle' and accompanied her Paupau to the market and to church. She attended confession every week despite feeling as though she had to make sins up just to have something to confess to Mr Father Priest. She even attended classes to prepare her for her Confirmation and regurgitated whatever her Confirmation teacher would want to hear even though she knew deep down she didn't believe in any of it. She always happily offered to do the dishes after dinner, took out the rubbish and helped her Paupau around the house. At home she was an obedient and considerate 'good girl', albeit a little clumsy and sometimes outspoken. That was who she was at home with her Hong Kongese Catholic family.

The girl didn't know how or when it happened, but outside the confines of her family cocoon she began to lead a very different life. Her mother had chosen to provide the girl with a Western education, which came with lots of positives—open encouragement of a child's creative expression, critical thinking, a sense of self-worth and confidence—but it also exposed the girl to all the negatives which were often associated with international schools. Over-confidence, an outsized sense of personal entitlement, right to privacy, mixed-gender parties, smoking, drinking, drugs and sex—a Hong Kongese mother's worst nightmare.

In the beginning it was nothing more criminal than curiosity. The girl wondered what another life might be like, one in which she could break free from playing the tiresome role as the perfect daughter. At first it was nothing major—a few embellishments of the truth here, a little white lie there. Then she began to lie to her family about where she was, whom she was with and what she was doing. Before realizing it, she had spiralled into a full-on embrace of a double life that by definition was kept secret from her whole family.

At the same time, the girl adored school. Deep down she was a complete nerd—she loved books, writing, learning and tests. What made her love school even more was when she saw how her mother and Paupau would look up to her Auntie Yin, and how they took her opinions seriously on almost all matters. The girl decided she would be an educated person. *Education is what will make people take me seriously.* She respected her family for valuing it and believed that if she was as educated as her Auntie Yin, her family would be proud of her and take her seriously.

But spending time at an international school with wealthy expat classmates exposed her to more than just an education. She coveted their way of life— how they were able to express their meta-narratives through their clothes and hairstyles, how their parents seemed so lax about expectations and rules, and how confident these classmates seemed about their sense of self.

Most of her classmates were heavily influenced by the music they listened to at the time. Some were into Nirvana and the whole grunge scene whilst others like Dominic lived for Metallica and the Prodigy. Many of the girls in her year were mad for the Backstreet Boys and Spice Girls. *Why can't I do that too? Why can't I dress the way I want, paint my nails and dye my hair? Why do I have to look like such a total nerd?*

Slowly the girl began to make tiny adjustments. She started rummaging through the family sewing kit to extract as many safety pins as she could. She stuffed them into her school uniform skirt pocket and as soon as she got onto the school bus, she pinned them into her tights. She decided to interpret the school uniform code loosely by wearing trainers, painting her nails black and wearing her school tie by her chest. When the older girls in Year Ten and Eleven had drawn tattoo patterns on their arms, she did the same, covering forearms in black biro that often smudged all over her uniform by the time she got home.

Whenever her Paupau would ask why she was such a dirty mess she would lie and say she got ink on her from art class.

By the time she was twelve she had smoked her first cigarette. It was more out of sheer curiosity than anything else that spurred her to slip one of her mother's Salem Menthol Lights into her pocket and smoke it in the fire stairwell behind their flat before school. *Yuck. This is pretty gross!* she thought, but she persevered. Before long she was buying her own fags. With a pack costing only 30HKD at the time and Circle K's lack of an ID policy for guais, it was easier to buy her own cigarettes than risk getting caught nabbing her mother's.

At thirteen she spent Friday evenings on the roof of Pacific Place—a high-end shopping mall complex—smoking cigarettes and hashish with peers older than her when she had told her mother she was out with female classmates at the cinema. *I'm not technically lying . . . I'm in the same mall as the cinema. I am with my girlfriends as I said I would be . . .* These were the types of justifications she told herself to help dilute her guilt.

The girl had become close with Lara—a girl in her year that she had known since primary school, but they only started to hang out together since they discovered they shared similar interests: smoking cigarettes, listening to heavy rock and drinking beers in broad daylight in Victoria Park. They would laugh every time scornful Hong Kongese mothers with their younger children tutted and shook their heads in judgmental disgust. The girl wondered if her mother had seen her this way if she would do the same.

When her mother thought she was out ice-skating, shopping or at a friend's house watching a PG13 film on the weekend, the girl was actually at a bar in Wan Chai with Lara and a few sixth-formers slamming tequila shots, playing pool and smoking. It wasn't the drinking nor the smoking that she enjoyed. Rather, it was doing something so completely different from what her family would ever expect of her, something so utterly outrageous that thrilled the girl. This thrill was like a drug and each time she tried to chase it, she found herself piling on another lie, and then another and another.

The girl didn't want to lie to her mother for the sake of being deceitful. She simply knew that if her mother found out what she had really been up to, not only would she pull her daughter out of the school immediately, it would also break her.

In Hong Kong culture a girl would already be considered to be 'bad' or 'rotten' for simply smoking cigarettes. Who she was as a person, how much she helped around the house, how good her grades were or how much she loved her family wouldn't matter. She was a bad rotten girl. So the notion that this bad rotten girl would also be drinking, mixing with boys and smoking cannabis would be an abomination.

What Mum doesn't know won't hurt her. I could never tell her what I've been up to . . . she won't get why I do it. She'll just get angry and she'll hate me . . . she'll be so hurt. She reasoned. Sometimes it was better for a mother to live in the illusion that her daughter was a perfect little girl. It was the only way to protect her.

'When will I be going?' asked the girl.

'Next year. Form Three. Good time. Before GCSE. You do Hong Kong way.'

'Oh.' Her heart sank. Her eyes darted back and forth, trying to process what was being instructed. 'But I don't want to go. Mum, I don't want to go, I can't. I'll be leaving my friends!' exclaimed the girl.

She thought of her friends, of Lara, of Dominic, of her wicked Friday and Saturday nights of mischief. What would happen to her freedom? What would happen to them?

'Friends you see on weekends. Make new friends. Better friends. Girls from St. Paul and Marymount, they good girls. Make good friends for you. Friends who study hard.'

'But, Mum, my friends, my school, my life? What about my life? This is my life!' she screeched as it dawned on her that she was being handed a life without her friends, a life of strict school rules, knee-length skirts, no makeup, no eyeliner, no black nail varnish or Vans. It was a harsh sentence, disproportionate to all the crimes she actually had committed, let alone to the ones she feared her mother knew about.

'You make new friends, have new life in new school. This not your life to decide. This for me to decide. You go to new school. New government school.'

Her mother's words were razor sharp. The girl couldn't accept a life of conformity; her life at home was already that way, and now faced with having her only means of release taken away from her, the girl was crushed.

Her mother let out a big sigh.

'Listen to me, your school fees too expensive. I cannot afford. You too expensive, cost too much,' said the mother as she clasped the girl's hands in between hers. 'Please. Please follow my way and try to understand. Please go to government school. Cheaper, better education—correct education. Teach you correct way.'

'But Mum, my life! You can't just take my life away like that. You can't!' It was the first time the girl had ever protested against her mother's direct wishes.

'Please, I ask you. Please follow my way,' beseeched her mother, her eyes begging for her daughter to obey and accept her mother's decision. It was the first time she had ever heard her mother say please like that. She couldn't recall a time when her mother implored her daughter to do anything. Realising this, the girl's heart tugged. She knew her school fees were extortionate, and the only way her mother had been able to continue paying them was through immense sacrifice. *How can I say no to my mother after all that she has done for me? She has given up so much, sacrificed so much of herself for me, to send me to some fancy international school. How can I say no?* The girl thought about all the luxuries her mother had lavished on her since she could remember, luxuries that modest families like theirs couldn't afford without immense hard work. Realising this, the girl felt spoilt and ungrateful. She knew she could not reject her mother's request and yet again would have to play obligingly the role of a dutiful daughter. Refusing her mother would mean further sacrifices and the girl could not bear living with that guilt. As she came to terms with her potential new life, she was reminded of the quote she had scribbled into her journal despite not fully appreciating Kundera's work at that age. *'If a mother was Sacrifice personified, then a daughter was Guilt, with no possibility of redress.'* – Milan Kundera, *The Unbearable Lightness of Being.*

That Monday her mother wrote out a list of things the girl needed to 'fix' in preparation for her three-hour entrance exam to either St. Paul's or Marymount. First was the girl's terrible Maths performance. Despite being a keen learner, the girl was somewhat mathematically challenged. Her mother quickly found a university graduate called Stephanie who was a twenty-minute walk from their home and willing to take on the monster of a challenge—to bring the girl's Maths level up to Hong Kong standards.

'Let's just see what level you're on first. Complete the following exercises.'

Stephanie handed the girl a photocopied worksheet.

'I'm in my top set in Maths at school,' the girl announced proudly, but as soon as she laid eyes on the gibberish before her, she wished she could eat her words.

'I'll give you ten minutes.'

'Okay.'

But it wasn't okay. She scowled and scrunched her face for the next ten minutes, staring down at the paper. She could not write a single thing down.

'Is there nothing you can answer?' sighed Stephanie, shocked that the girl had left the whole sheet blank. The girl lowered her head and shook it in embarrassment.

'Well, we have a lot of work to do. This paper I just gave you was taken from a Primary Five Mathematics textbook at a Hong Kong school. That is three years <u>below</u> your grade.'

Stephanie looked dumfounded as she shook her head and let out a big sigh.

The girl wanted to burst into tears. She had never felt so utterly stupid and incompetent before. It wasn't Stephanie's fault. *Year Five! I can't even do Maths at a ten-year-old's level! How did I get into top-set Maths if I suck? How does that make any sense?* Thoughts expressed only to herself as she clenched her fists and began her first gruelling Maths session. The girl never thought herself a particularly smart child, but she never entertained the notion that she was all-out stupid until that afternoon.

For the next three months the girl attended every single Maths session, completed all her extra homework and worked hard to bring her level up to expectations. She didn't do it to get into her mother's chosen schools; she did it for herself. She wanted to prove to herself and to a very patient Stephanie that she wasn't completely incompetent. *I am not completely stupid. I cannot be completely rubbish. I am not incompetent. I'll prove it. I have to prove it.* She detested every session but went through with it anyway.

Next on her mother's list was for the girl to take up French. Both schools required students to have an aptitude for a second language and seeing as French was their preferred choice, her mother enrolled the girl at the Alliance Française Learning Centre in Wan Chai. Every Saturday morning the girl took the MTR on her own for two hours of intensive French lessons. She listened, she made notes, she answered questions, she completed her homework assignments and did her tests. She did as she was told.

At first, she resented the lifestyle: having to stay home on a Friday night, having to get up early on Saturday morning instead of getting a lie-in, having to sit in a French class with fifteen adult learners and having no one her age to talk to. But she was obligated, because in Hong Kong culture when your mother asks you to do something, or in this case begs you, you don't refuse, you simply do it whether you want to or not. Every time she wanted to throw her hands up and say 'Fuck it', she reminded herself of her expensive school fees and how hard her mother had had to work to pay them. *You need to do this. You've started anyway.*

Third on the list was for the daughter to become an altar girl. Her mother figured that as both schools were Catholic, being an altar girl would swing the odds in her favour at being accepted.

'Really? Do I really need to do this?'

'Yes. Give you better chance. Be altar girl, Priest can write you nice recommendation letter to school, then school will accept you. Much better chance this way,' replied the mother.

The girl recoiled at the idea of donning the unflattering white gown and having to pretend for another audience. The girl wasn't even sure if she believed in God and assumed faith would be a natural prerequisite for being an altar girl. *Great, another show I need to play in.* But when the girl thought about it, she reasoned that she had been playing her different roles already with her double-life that one more wouldn't make a difference.

As soon as her Paupau heard her beloved granddaughter would be an altar girl, she was beaming with joy.

'You altar girl? Really? Wah! Such great news, so happy. This make me so happy. Thank Mr God and Mr Jesus. This is good for you, so good. See, Mr God bless you with this duty. Very good. The best news. The best.'

What else could the girl do but to nod in agreement and play along. She couldn't bear the thought of disappointing her Paupau, who had already begun calling her church friends to announce the blessed news.

Their priest was more than thrilled to welcome the mixed-race girl to his team of young eager Catholics, so keen that it didn't matter that she couldn't read Cantonese and was therefore unable to follow the order of service.

'Erh, Father, my daughter can't read Cantonese. Would that be an issue?' asked her mother in Cantonese.

'No, of course not. No need to worry about that. I've seen her at Mass every week since she was a baby, I'm sure she knows all of it by heart by now, don't you?'

The priest shrugged off any concerns her mother may have and patted the girl on her shoulder.

'Ummm. I guess . . .' replied the girl.

'See, it's okay. No problem. Doesn't matter can't read Cantonese, she'll be trained on what to do and I'm sure she'll be able to follow along.'

The priest patted the girl on the back and gestured for one of the senior girls to help get the girl fitted for a new altar gown. But it did matter. It mattered to the girl who felt utterly stupid in her new white altar gown. It mattered every week when the girl was sat up behind the altar in front of an audience of worshippers as she pretended to be able to read along characters of adoration and praise to a God she didn't know if she believed in. She felt like a fake, a hypocrite, a liar— what was worse was that she was lying to herself, and she hated it.

When she was quickly promoted to be the frankincense holder, she felt even more ridiculous about the whole charade and wished for it to come to an end soon. But every time she was up there and looked at her Paupau, all that went away. None of it mattered because it made her Paupau so happy. *Look at Paupau. She is so happy; she is so proud of me. Do it for Paupau. Paupau is happy, that's all that matters.*

Before she knew it, the entrance exams came, and it was time for the girl to put all that hard work, time and money to the test and make her mother proud.

'Put this on,' instructed the mother.

Her mother had laid out an outdated light blue cotton collared M&S dress and matching shoes for her daughter, a dress she had not worn in years, not because she had outgrown it in size but in taste.

'Really?' the girl scowled.

'Yes, put it on.'

'But Mum, it's so uncool. It'll make me look—'

'You not going for fashion show,' interrupted her mother. 'You going there for exam. Must set good impression. Must show them you mean business.'

'Yes, but it's not an interview, just an exam. They won't be looking at what I'm wearing. They'll be looking at what I'm writing.'

'I don't care. You wear dress. Look respectable.'

Three hours. One hour each for each paper—English, Mathematics and French. One paper after the other, no breaks. She did it, <u>twice</u>. Once at St. Paul's and then again, a few days later, at Marymount. She had sat various tests and assessments at school but nothing longer than an hour. Her teachers always reminded her class that it wasn't always the result that mattered but the learning journey, and if the result wasn't quite as expected, it was the effort that counted. She had never sat an exam like this before—being one of many single desks lost within rows and rows of girls lined up in a grand assembly hall, where the results were the only thing that counted to get a foot in the door.

As soon as the exams were over, the girl decided to put all that exam prep behind her. After all, there was nothing left to be done except to wait for her results. She was relieved that she could return to her secret rebellious social life and figured if she were to be accepted to one of those schools, it would mean the end to all that, so she'd better make the most of it whilst she still could.

All seemed as though it had returned to normal. Until she was sat down after school one afternoon by her mother and instructed to read aloud both letters of rejection. Both letters may as well have been written by the same person—the same stoic tone telling the girl that she did not meet the required standards.

Whilst your daughter was highly recommended by Father Lam, it is with regret that we must decline your daughter's application to our institution.

The girl put the letters down on the dining table and looked up at her mother, face scrunched up, ready for a verbal beating.

'See. Must be bad math score. Your math so bad. They don't teach you proper in ESF school. Too relaxed.'

Her mother shook her head.

'What happens now?' the girl asked in earnest.

'Now,' sighed the mother. 'Now I have to pay your school fees.' Another deep sigh.

The disappointment the girl experienced that day wasn't that she didn't get in. She was thrilled not to have to attend a preppy school with a ridiculous discipline code and uniform and be sentenced to a life without her friends and their unruly way of having fun. No. The disappointment she felt was in herself. She could have sabotaged her exams. She could have slacked her way through her Maths tuition. She could have showed up half-asleep to her French lessons. She could have left her exam transcripts blank or written gibberish. But she didn't. She had done none of those things. Rather, the girl truly tried her best not just out of guilt and obligation to her mother but because she was adamant at proving to herself and to her mother that she wasn't incompetent. But sometimes your best just isn't good enough.

FIFTEEN

TEQUILA BUS RIDE

'Here, drink this.'

Dominic hands her a slightly battered bottle of water. The girl, thirteen years old, looks at it, a little confused.

'Erh, I'm not thirsty. And your water looks weird.'

She notices the slightly yellow tinge of Dominic's 'water'.

'It's not water. It's tequila. You tried it before?'

'No. Why's it in a water bottle?'

'So no one would suspect.'

'Oh.'

'Have a sip. See if you like it.'

He hands her the bottle and without hesitation she takes a sip, careful not to spill any of it on her school uniform. The tequila leaves a trail of fire down her throat as her body feels warm and alive. Whilst she doesn't care too much for its taste, the burning sensation excites her as she takes sip after sip.

'Hey! Easy. Not too much. You'll get fucked.'

Dominic grabs the bottle off her.

'Dominic . . . why have you got tequila with you, at school?'

''Cause Mona dumped me and then I had a Physics exam today.'

'Oh.'

'More?' he asks with a wink.

'Just a little.'

Some bus rides are more memorable than others. That was one of them—being only thirteen and feeling outrageously rebellious, drinking tequila on the school bus home.

SIXTEEN

YOU'RE GOING TO HELL

Despite failing her entrance exams, the girl continued with her altar girl duties. The joy that beamed from her Paupau's face each week at Mass was sufficient motivation for her to play make-believe with God.

Six months into her altar girl duties she was put forward to assist at the Easter Vigil Evening Mass. Her Paupau was thrilled that her beloved granddaughter would join the other ten altar boys and girls in serving God. What an honour it was indeed! The girl was given the grand responsibility of holding the Paschal Candle. Being larger than the other Hong Kongese altar girls, her larger than average size as per Hong Kong standards was perfect for such a physical task.

The Easter Vigil Mass started as it always did with a procession of the Paschal Candle. The church was packed wall to wall with anticipating devoted Catholics all sweltering in the April humid heat. All air conditioning and fans were turned off to protect the 'light of Christ' which did nothing to protect one's senses from the array of odours emitted by the congregation.

Maybe it was something she had eaten earlier, or perhaps it was the heat. Maybe it was the terrible stench of armpits and feet, or perhaps it was her nerves. But as soon as the procession began, she felt her tummy rumble and bubble. Someone had switched on the blender in her guts. *Don't fart. You cannot fart in church. Not here, not now.* All she had to do was get through raising the Paschal Candle three times and it would be over. *Just get through this. It will be okay. You can do this.*

Raise one. 'The light of Christ,' uttered the congregation in unison. The pain in her gut did not subside. Cramps started to build up. *No. Hold it together. Not here, not now. Everyone is watching you. You can do this.*

Raise two. 'The light of Christ.'

The candle felt heavier this time. The church somehow felt even hotter as her abdomen swelled and cramps grew stronger. *Get it together. Squeeze your butt! Squeeze! You're not embarrassing yourself in front of all these people. They'll hear you, they'll definitely smell you! You can do this.*

Raise three. 'The light of Christ.'

The candle wobbled, ever so slightly, on its way towards God. Someone in the congregation gasped. The girl was about to lose all composure. The beads of sweat turned to trickles now streaming down her face and back. Her trousers underneath grew tighter, contracting with every breath. Bubbles and rumbles of painful cramps continued. *This isn't a fart. Oh my God! This isn't a fart! I need to shit. I need to SHIT! Don't shit yourself. You cannot shit yourself here. Not in a white robe. Not here. Not now. Oh my God! HELP!*

The procession ended, and the girl was comforted by the fact that she was now out of the spotlight but was dying to relieve herself. *Squeeze your butt! You are not spraying shit all over that plastic chair! Not in church! You can't! No way!* She pulled all sorts of faces, rocked her body forwards and backwards, left and right, all in a vain attempt to keep her bowel contents inside. *Oh dear! Oh shit! Literally SHIT!* She felt it. The warm ooze of utter horrific humiliation. She desperately wanted to hide, to disappear, but it was too late. Suddenly she sprang out of her seat, mumbled to the altar boy next to her that she was going to throw up and dashed out of the church. She lied. She lied in church, in the presence of the priest and the whole congregation and to an altar boy during Easter Vigil Mass.

But she couldn't think of that now. All she could think about was not tripping over her white robe as she sprinted to the toilet. She had made a mess of her pale blue daisy printed knickers. *Phew.* Luckily nothing got on her trousers or robe.

'What happened? You okay?'

Her Paupau must have seen her dash out of the church.

'Yes, Paupau. I'm okay. I just wasn't feeling so well. I felt sick,' she assured her Paupau through the toilet door.

'Must be too hot inside.'

'Yes. Must be too hot.'

She didn't want to disclose her embarrassingly shameful secret to Paupau that she shat her pants in front of an audience of two hundred and then went on to lie to the boy next to her to save face.

But then things can always get worse, and they did. *Where's the toilet paper? Why's there no toilet paper? ARGH! Oh my God! You have got to be joking! Is this for lying? It is, isn't it? I'm being punished for lying.* The girl had no choice but to wipe herself with her socks and go commando.

The girl sheepishly stepped out of the cubicle. Paupau saw the girl's complexion and decided to take the girl home. It was the only time Paupau had ever cut a Mass short in her entire life.

'We go home. Not feeling well, better go home. Too hot inside,' Paupau comforted her.

All the way home the girl's jeans chafed against her butt cheeks, each step reminding her of her humiliation. It was the longest thirty-minute walk of her short life.

As soon as the girl got back, she dashed into the shower to wash off her shame. She couldn't believe she had shat herself, let alone that she had done it in church. She wondered if anyone knew or would find out, and if they did, how on earth she'd be able to live that down.

Paupau made her some hot tea as the girl lay on the black leather sofa, wishing for the day, the evening, her existence, to end.

'You feeling better now? Okay now?'

Her Paupau brushed her head and took her temperature with her hand—Paupau never needed a thermometer, it was a special power that she possessed in her hands; she could always tell accurately, just through touch, if someone had a fever or not.

'No fever, must be feeling better,' confirmed Paupau.

'Yes, Paupau. A bit better now.'

The girl looked up at her Paupau and caught sight of the crucifix that hung in the living room.

You're going to Hell, you know that right? You shat your pants and you lied in church. Then you lied to your Paupau. Lying about smoking and drinking is one thing, but this—this is the worst. You actually lied inside a church when God is supposed to be watching, on like one of the holiest nights. Lying in church – you're going to Hell, she thought to herself.

SEVENTEEN

MORE LIKE SUSANNA

'Why can't you be more like Susanna?' Her mother sighed at the girl.

But she couldn't be more like Susanna. Even if she tried. She wanted to badly, desperately—God, did she want to.

Susanna was half Caucasian and half Hong Kongese but in so many ways was so different from the girl. Susanna with the perfect posture, slender athletic figure, the long silky brown hair, the perfect manners. Susanna who spoke softly and sweetly, with fluttering eyelashes and a cute smile.

The girl looked up at her mother and met the disappointment she saw with frustration of her own. Could her mother not see? Could she not see that her mother had asked the one question that she should never ask her daughter? Could her mother not tell that she was asking for her daughter to become someone else? Could her mother not foretell that those words would haunt her for many years to come?

The girl continued to hold her mother's gaze as she attempted to convey how hurt she was by those sour words. But nothing got through. Instead her mother repeated the question, rubbing salt in the wound.

'Why? Why can't you be more like her? Huh? She is so sweet. She speaks so sweetly. Sweet words, sweet smile—many people like Susanna. Not like you. You? You're so rough, so direct. Too rough—not sweet like her. You must learn from her. Learn how to be like her.'

Those words were acid and as she swallowed them, they had begun to burn a hole through the girl's confidence—a hole that would grow bigger and deeper. *If being more like Susanna would mean my mother would like me more, then I guess I'll just have to try and be like her*, thought the fourteen-year-old girl.

The girl concluded that if she was to be more like Susanna, she would first need to look like her. So, one evening she decided to study her naked body in the bathroom mirror. She had to stand on the toilet seat to get a full-length view of herself. She had seen herself naked thousands of times, but it had never occurred to her until then to <u>really</u> look at herself. *If I am more like Susanna maybe Mum would like me better. Maybe the boys at school would stop teasing me for being such a tomboy. Maybe they would even fancy me . . . and give me a second glance.*

As she examined her body, words she never thought she would ever associate with herself sprang up one after the other. *I don't see a Susanna; I only see me. I don't see a Susanna . . . I only see <u>me</u>. And all I see is an ugly, fat, frizzy-haired tomboy! I don't see a Susanna; I only see <u>me</u>. Why can't I look more like Susanna? Why?* That was the first time the girl ever cried in the shower.

She had never compared herself to another girl before—it never occurred to her that it mattered, but suddenly it did. It was <u>all</u> that mattered. She had never been ashamed of her appearance, of her body or who she was before. Now, it was all she could think about.

Why can't you be more like Susanna? Those words looped in her mind all the way through the rest of Year Nine. The girl wondered if her mother knew that Susanna was as mean as she was beautiful. Susanna who would blank the girl every time they crossed paths in the school corridor whenever Susanna was with the 'popular' crew and then switch to being the girl's closest friend when it was convenient to Susanna. The same Susanna who had been friends with the girl since they were small children and all the way through primary school. Susanna who would join in with Ranj and the rugby team in sniggering at the girl because of her cheap clothes, because she was fat, because of her greasy frizzy hair, because she was 'frigid', because she was a tomboy, because . . . well, just because. Susanna who would venture out to Repulse Bay Beach on Friday nights, booze up on sugary alcopops and in her intoxicated state get close and personal with the same boys who taunted the girl. But none of that mattered, because she was Susanna, perfection personified.

A few months had passed since her mother's atomic question and the girl decided that she both couldn't and didn't want to be more like Susanna. She decided she could only be more like herself, and at fourteen that meant being the complete opposite of what Susanna was. Her mother wanted demure; she became abrasive. Her mother wanted polite; she became even more outspoken to the point of being rude. Her mother wanted calm and pristine; she became loud, brash and rebellious—all hidden from her mother's and Paupau's view of course. Her new rebellious streak made her 'cool'. She had gone from being the bushy-eyebrowed chubby geek to skater chick with her baggy jeans and lumberjack shirt. Suddenly the girl was friends with an older crowd, and she didn't have to care that Ranj and the rugby jocks still make fun of her. Suddenly she was no longer the disco loner with no one to dance with but was joined by classmates who'd rather sit on the steps outside with her and have a spitball competition than slow-dance inside.

But it wasn't enough to deafen those words. In her defiance against all things Susanna, she had unknowingly stopped herself from being seen as a fourteen-year-old girl and taken her tomboy role too far with her penis doodles, fart jokes, love for action and horror films, and a mouth for elaborate profanities. Having already been rebellious since Year Eight, all of this had come so naturally to her. But being seen solely as the cool tomboy wasn't something she had been expecting.

'You're like a sister to us, but cooler! We couldn't ever talk like this to another girl. You're super cool. You're one of us! One of the lads!' her new guy friends would say.

It wasn't what she wanted. She didn't want to be 'one of the lads', or like a 'sister' to them—those were the kind of girls you would never fancy. She realised her plan had backfired and was desperate for a chance to fix it.

Not before long the perfect opportunity came in the form of a residential trip to Zhuhai as part of their Mandarin class. *This is it—this is my chance to show them I'm not just a tomboy.* The girl snuck her mother's black jersey shirt and black lace bra into her bag and told herself that if they could see her out of her usual baggy shirt and jeans and in some more feminine clothing, they would see her as a girl—a fanciable girl with 'parts n' all'.

It was well past lights out. The girl had donned her mother's black shirt, deliberately leaving the top three buttons undone to proudly show off her ample black-laced breasts. She was one of the few girls in her year to have developed so voluptuously and knew it would definitely get the boys' attention. Dolled up in Susanna's makeup, they and some other classmates snuck into Ranj and Matt's hotel room.

'Let's spice this party up and play Truth or Dare!' Ranj piped up. He had been ogling the girl's chest since she had walked in.

'Oh my God! I love Truth or Dare! Don't you?' clapped Susanna as she squeezed next to Matt on the floor.

'You want one?' offered Matt, holding out an open pack of Marlboro Lights. He had managed to sneak in a pack of fags along with some beers from the hotel lobby.

'Sure, thanks.'

'Oh my GOD! I didn't know <u>you smoked</u>?' shrieked Susanna. She was beside herself with the fervent outrage of a true hypocrite.

'Yeah, she does. Didn't you know?' said Matt. 'Where've you been, Susanna? She's been smoking hash with Lara's brother every Friday night whilst you're down at the beach.'

'OH MY GOD! YUCK! That's disgusting. Eww,' repulsed Susanna in a characteristically perfect pantomime of moral indignation.

Susanna wasn't disgusted that the girl was smoking. Susanna was jealous that the girl had stolen her double-life thunder by being more 'grown up', more badass, more rebellious than she was. The girl smirked and lit her cigarette.

They played Truth or Dare. At that age, it was the coolest game—a game to prove how grown up you were, how cool you were, how gutsy you were. At that age, you don't think of it as a game that would normalise being kissed, groped, licked, locked in a wardrobe with a boy whether you liked him or not. No. You don't think of things like that at the time. You don't think of it as a game that would teach teenage girls that if you were given a dare you didn't agree to do, you couldn't just back out and say no. Because saying no would be breaking the rules, saying no would make you uncool, frigid, a reject. No. And if you were one of the girls who preferred to play it safe and chose 'truth', you'd be labelled a wimp, a wuss, someone that wasn't fun. What does it teach teenage girls when you tell them that the truth isn't welcome? What does it teach them when they see that silence and non-consent is preferred to the 'oh you're so boring' truth? No. You don't think of this at fourteen. You don't think of it as a game that would stigmatise the notion of consent.

To the girl at the time, it was her chance for the rugby team to see her, to fancy her, 'parts n' all'. It didn't take much. The poorly fitted shirt squeezed her chest so tightly that it nearly caused her tits to burst out. She was, or they were, the centre of attention.

Ranj was dared to take the girl's glasses off her face, fold them, put them down her cleavage and take them out again. A gentleman would use his fingertips and gingerly insert her glasses between her breasts. A gentleman would ask for permission before doing anything and check that she would be okay with it. But Ranj was no gentleman—he had already badmouthed her to all his friends.

Ranj pulled her glasses off her face, stuffed them down her chest as his chubby fingers groped hungrily at her breasts, squeezing at everything he could find before pulling her glasses back out. As he turned around, his penis stood erect underneath his sweatpants. Matt spat out his beer and the rest of them sniggered.

All except for her. *Why is that funny? Why am I not laughing? Was I supposed to be okay with that? Is it okay that I'm not okay with that?* Mixed feelings. Feeling both aroused and violated. But she told herself if she wanted to be seen as a girl, if she wanted to be fancied, if she wanted to be like Susanna, she would have to silence her ambivalence. She told herself it was fine, that she didn't need to make a fuss, that she was cool and could play along, that it was just a game. So, she said nothing, and she learnt to accept the rules imposed upon her.

Later that year during the end of Year Nine camp, the girl found herself standing outside around the back of her camp hut in nothing but a towel. Ranj had called for her. She had just come out of the shower and not thinking much of it, she wrapped herself in a towel and went outside to speak with him. In her mind, it was perfectly innocent. After all, Ranj had seen her in far less during swimming lessons when she had to walk around the school pool in nothing but a thin bathing suit.

'You wanna meet me out here after the BBQ?' he said, caressing her shoulder, and smiled.

'Yeah, sure. Is Matt coming with you? I'll ask Susanna if she wants to join.'

'No. Just you and me, right here. After the BBQ.' Toothy smile.

'Oh. Okay,' she replied.

She knew Ranj fancied her, especially ever since the Zhuhai tit-grope. She wasn't sure if she fancied Ranj and was pretty sure she didn't—she hadn't forgotten what he had said about her but figured as he was one of the more popular boys in her year, she should just go along with it. *I guess it's okay to hang out with him. He's okay, I guess.*

But it wasn't okay. It wasn't okay when he met her later, after the BBQ, in a place where no one else was around. It wasn't okay when he jabbed his tongue down her throat and washing-machined her mouth mid-sentence. At first, she said nothing and did nothing, telling herself it was her choice to have met up with him behind her hut that evening as planned. *Learn to play by the rules. He's into you, he likes you, this is the force of his affection, not his aggression.* But it wasn't okay when he pushed her against the hut wall so strongly that she scraped her elbows and hit her head. She told herself this was what they were supposed to do, that this was their first date. *Learn to play by the rules. He's into you, he likes you. This is what girls do—drive boys to violent passion.* But it wasn't okay that he began to dry hump her, thrusting his erect dick against her thin cycling shorts. *No, this is not okay.* She pushed him so hard that Ranj lost balance and fell over onto his ass.

'What the hell?' he yelled.

'Sorry, you okay? Shit. Sorry,' she chuckled.

'What the fuck? What's wrong with you?'

'I'm just not ready for that . . . sorry.'

'So why the hell did you ask for it then?'

'What? I didn't ask for it!'

'Yes, you did. This afternoon, you came out in your towel, then now you came to meet me out here.'

'What? I came out in a towel earlier because I was in the shower when the girls said you were outside. I came to meet you because you invited me. And besides, you've seen me in a swimsuit?'

'You're a frigid cock-tease, you know that?'

'Not this again!'

'I thought you were cool. At least you pretend to be. Fuck this. This isn't going to work.'

'What the fuck? What isn't going to work? Were we even a couple? What d'you mean?'

But before she could even finish asking him, he had left. She had no idea they were even a couple; it was all news to her. This was the second time Ranj had dumped her for being 'frigid'. This time Dominic wasn't there to console her; he was far, far away at university. *Would Susanna have let it happen? Would she have let Ranj dry hump her against a wall? Why can't I just be like Susanna?*

The girl would continue to ask those questions all the way through to the end of the summer holidays when one of her school friends held a birthday party. The usual gang was there—the rugby boys, Susanna and a couple of others. The same skinny Minnies standing in their tiny skirts and tank tops hugging flat waists and flat chests, propped up in high-heeled clogs, framed by flat-ironed hair. The same girls who'd flick their hair, giggle and sip alcopops disguised as sodas through pink straws as the boys sat in front of them pretending not to be eyeballing them and hiding their hard-ons.

It was same shitty party set-up, but this time, the girl decided to make one more attempt to be seen as a girl. It would be her last chance before she moved to Paris the following week. *This is my only chance to prove to them I can look like a girl, that I can be like them.*

She thought she looked fantastic—fitted black jeans, fitted shirt, high heels and make-up courtesy of her mother. *I look hot! I look amazing.* But that was until Ranj, whose ego was still bruised, caught a glimpse of the girl and quacked with forced laughter. Pointing, laughing, shaking his head—everything to take revenge on the girl for the hut incident.

'Do you see this? HA-HA-HA! What are you doing? HA-HA-HA! You're so trash!'

Ranj pointed at her and continued to force laughter. The other boys as if on cue followed their leader and joined in. They didn't know what they were laughing at nor why, they merely imitated Ranj as he hedged his rejection by insulting her.

'HA-HA-HA! You're so trash! Come on, who are you fooling? You trying to look sexy? Really? Come on! Fat ass!' Ranj continued whilst the others smirked.

'That's right, fat ass! HAHAHAHA,' the boys laughed. The same boys who last month shared smokes with her and called her cool.

The girl couldn't move. Their roaring teases felt like a multitude of punches on her body as she felt all the air inside her escape. The girl who had once been so quick to spew out profanities stood there in silence as she scanned the room full of distorted faces, looking for an ally to help her. Her eyes met with Susanna's. Susanna, whom her mother wanted her so much to be like, not only didn't stop the boys from mocking her, but joined in. Susanna, who had been friends with the girl since they were little children, joined in and giggled as the boys continued to call her names. The girl pictured their laughing heads exploding and their brains spraying all over her. She was enraged—bruised that the boys continued to throw words like TRASH, TRAMP, FAT and FRIGID at her, livid that her childhood friend would betray her and incensed that she was just standing there and taking it.

Her friends had completely shamed her, left her utterly humiliated, all because she had tried to act like a 'normal teenage girl', whatever the fuck that means. *More like Susanna? I don't fucking think so.*

I want to leave, to go somewhere where I should be really in my place, where I would fit in . . . but my place is nowhere; I am unwanted.

— *Jean-Paul Sartre, Nausea*

PART II

When you're a teenager, no matter how monstrously you fuck up, you always believe there will be someone there to help fix things for you.

EIGHTEEN

GEORGES

The girl's mother fed her daughter a very specific diet of words—one that taught her that complete self-reliance was the only way to ensure one's sense of stability and security in life. Her mother taught her that she should never depend on a man, any man; that she should always have her own money, her own property, her own life. Her mother taught her that relying on a man is dangerous because that man can and will leave at any point. And if the girl didn't do as she was taught, she'd be left with no money, no home, no life.

To the girl these lessons made sense, after all her own father had left her to be raised by a household of women—strong independent women. To the girl the idea that they needed a man at home or in their lives was just odd.

So, it came as a surprise to the girl when her mother began dating a French Caucasian twelve years her senior called Georges who frequented Hong Kong often on business trips. It wasn't the first time her mother had a 'special friend' but it was the first time her mother appeared to be in a committed relationship since her marriage to the girl's father. Aside from Mr Harry, whom the girl hadn't heard from since she was around eleven, her mother had not introduced any of her boyfriends or lovers to her daughter until Georges was invited to join them for a family dinner. This is a big deal, especially in Hong Kong culture, you don't just bring home any boyfriend or lover unless it was serious.

Georges seemed pleasant enough, albeit considered rude for not having touched much of Paupau's cooking which she had offered wholeheartedly.

'What is the matter with him? Why he no eat? Is he sick? He so skinny, look like have cancer! Ay-yah,' protested Paupau.

In their culture, not gobbling every morsel of food offered into one's bowl by the matriarch was considered very bad manners and disrespectful. To Paupau, this was a bad sign and this heavily influenced how the girl felt about Georges. *He's a bit of a weirdo. Why didn't he touch Paupau's food? Who doesn't like Chinese food? It's just food! Weirdo.* The girl thought as she couldn't help but compare him with Mr Harry. *Mr Harry was so much fun. He loved to laugh and eat but this guy . . . he looks so serious.* To her, Georges looked like stern stick-figure.

'He just doesn't like Chinese food, that's all,' defended the girl's mother.

'What you mean no liking Chinese food? Everybody love Chinese food. How can he have Chinese wife and no liking Chinese food? Ha? How? Not possible,' tutted Paupau as she shook her head disapprovingly.

But it was possible, for in a few years they decided to get married. What surprised the girl wasn't having to acknowledge her mother as a sexual being but to accept that her mother would become someone's Mrs So-and-so.

'Erh, I have a question to ask you,' interrupted the girl's mother one afternoon after school. The girl was busying herself with her homework so she could meet up with Lara later. 'What do you think of Georges?'

'What d'you mean? Erm, I guess he's okay . . .'

'Do you like him?'

'What d'you mean do I like him? I guess, erm, I dunno . . . I mean he's a bit weird. Like, he doesn't like Chinese food, that's weird.'

'But you like him?'

'Yeah, sure, I guess. Whatever,' huffed the girl impatiently. 'Mum, I've got homework so, erm . . .'

'So, what would you say if I marry him? Would you say it was a good idea?'

The girl paused and put her pen down.

'I dunno.'

'Well, what you think?'

'I dunno. I guess . . . I dunno. Why are you asking me anyway?'

'I want to know what you think. So, what you say? It good idea or not?' pressured the mother.

She didn't know why her mother was asking for her opinion and told herself that the questions must have been purely speculative.

'Yeah, I guess . . .' The girl shrugged. 'Now can I get back to my homework, please?'

Her mother would often throw all sorts of hypothetical conversations at the girl that she had figured this was just one of them. The girl did not guess that this was her mother's way of seeking the girl's blessing.

Her mother became Mrs Georges So-and-so in a civil ceremony at City Hall. The girl wore a pantsuit instead of a dress to her mother's disappointment. Dresses were for celebrations, and this, for the girl, wasn't one. She contemplated how odd it felt that in less than thirty minutes her mother had gone from an independent self-sufficient woman to Mrs So-and-so. *Will she keep her name?* Traditionally, married Hong Kongese women would keep their maiden name and only be known as 'Mrs' amongst friends. She had found it strange that women could so quickly change their names when they get married. *If you change your name and your name is your identity, does that mean you've changed your identity when you're married?* the girl pondered as she considered that perhaps this was what her mother was hoping for—to be able to shed herself of her past and embrace a future as a housewife Mrs So-and-so.

Whilst the girl understood her mother's need for companionship, she couldn't help but feel disappointed in her mother, that her mother was being a hypocrite for doing the very opposite of what she had instructed her daughter to do—now relying on yet another white man in order to give her some sense of status in a harsh and prejudiced world.

One day a few months into her marriage, the mother announced to the girl that they would be moving to Paris.

'No, not with Paupau and Auntie Yin. You and me. We move to Paris to live with Georges.'

It had been decided that as Mrs So-and-so, her mother ought to live where her husband lived. After all, Georges simply could not part with his four other children from two previous failed marriages—Sophie, Sebastian, Sonja and Sacha, despite spending more time in the year abroad than he did at home. But as Mrs So-and-so, she had to listen to her husband's request, uproot her fourteen-year-old daughter and establish a new life in Paris.

The prospect of leaving Hong Kong both terrified and excited the girl. She relished the idea of being able to leave her reputation as the fat tomboy behind her and reinvent herself. She, like her mother, could start a new persona, a new life—one in which she could be popular and cool. At the same time, she was anxious about living in a totally different country—new time zone, new culture, new language, new faces, new home. Home—she'd have to call somewhere else home, a place where she wouldn't have her Paupau. She dreaded the idea that she would be without her beloved Paupau who had raised her, who had been at every school bus drop-off and pick-up, who took her to all her ballet and piano lessons, who bought her whatever food she wanted, who had rubbed her feet when they ached from growing pains and soothed her tummy when she was unwell. Her Paupau, who made the best spicy noodles for breakfast, sung her Hakka folk songs and taught her how to play Hakka poker. *I cannot live without my Paupau.*

When the girl protested, her mother replied, 'I'm doing this for us, for you. To give you a new life, better life.'

'But I like the life I've got here. At home, in Hong Kong. Why can't I stay here?'

'You are my daughter. You must come with me, cannot stay here.'

'But Paupau could take care of me. I could just stay here.'

'No. Paupau is not your mother! I am your mother! You must go where I go. Besides Georges is my husband now and your stepfather. We must go and live where he lives.'

'So, just because you're married now means you need to move? And I need to move? I don't want to go. I want to stay here.'

'This is an order!'

The girl realised there was no point in arguing with her mother; the decision had already been made for her.

Up until now, despite their differences, the girl had always respected her mother. Sure, she had a mercurial nature, erratic temper and unpredictable giddy moods, but her mother had always championed being a strong, independent woman, who not only financially took care of the girl, but also her Auntie Yin and Paupau.

But things shifted the moment her mother decided to abandon this role and follow her husband to a foreign land in order to play Mrs So-and-so. This shift would wedge a distance between them, marking an erosion in a relationship that had already felt distant due to the many secrets the girl had kept from her mother.

In July 1998, they bid farewell to their pokey three bedroom flat and moved to a large barge by the River Seine in Paris. *This is going to be so strange.* The girl contemplated how everything was about to change. Up until now the girl had only lived amongst women in a small flat and never had to worry about hanging her bras and knickers to dry in the living room or walking around the flat in only her underwear during the sweltering summers. *There's going to be a man living with me, like an actual man. How awkward!*

The girl's reservations were briefly subdued when she arrived in Paris. The last time she was in Paris was with her mother and Auntie Yin on their way to the French Alps, so she recalled very little of her experience except that French people didn't seem to drink a lot of water and nothing was open on Sunday—not even an off-licence. It was a stark contrast from Hong Kong where water was easily accessible, and Sunday was the day for shopping and dining-out.

This city is phenomenal! It's so beautiful! Everything is so . . . wide! The girl was taken aback by how spaced out everything felt. Whereas in Hong Kong everything is stacked on top of each other, piled up and squeezed next to, Paris seemed so spacious. Everything looked and felt bigger—the grand wide boulevards that appeared never-ending, the palatial-looking Hussmann-style buildings with their signature second-floor balconies, even the trees looked bigger. This vast amount of space made Hong Kong's residential units look like prison cells.

When she arrived at her new home that overlooked both Bir Hakeim bridge and the Eiffel Tower, she was reminded of a film she used to watch with her mother. *Toto, we're not in Kansas anymore.*

THE UNBITABLE SANDWICH

I never considered myself as poor
not until this moment
when I take you out.
Wrinkled clear plastic
sandwich bag.
I hide you away
in shame
under my polyester blazer.
Judgemental sniggering rich kids.
Fancy backpacks with thick wallets.
Off to lunch in cafes.
But I hide you away
In shame
Under my cheap polyester blazer.
Square white bread
warm and soggy and smashed.
Flattened from
making war with books
in my oversized bag.
It's not a fancy backpack.
I hide you away
In shame
Under my cheap polyester blazer.

Your roast beef sliced too thick

Too much mustard.

I bite into you and leave

blood-stained teeth marks

from my swollen gums

on your bleached white wheat

for your inners will not submit

and whole slices of you slither out.

Yellow stains I cannot hide away

In shame

Now on my nasty polyester blazer.

Pieces of you flap about as I wrestle with you:

the unbitable sandwich

my mother packed.

Sent to torment me with embarrassment.

I never considered myself as poor

not until this moment

when I take you out,

my unbitable sandwich.

NINETEEN

LOSING IT TO AMERICAN HISTORY X

She had never been naive enough to believe she would lose her virginity to a husband. The idea of saving herself for her wedding night seemed naïve and juvenile, even somewhat unfair. *Why should I be expected to 'save myself' when Future Mr X would have probably stuck it in plenty others before me?* But on the other hand, she hadn't planned on losing her virginity at fifteen and with her very first boyfriend, Jason, whom she had met at her new school.

'You sure you want to do this?' asked Jason.

The glare of the TV playing *American History X* on VHS made his hazel eyes look grey.

'Yup. I am. Are you? I am if you are.'

She sat up on Jason's bed, feeling rather nervous. Both the girl and Jason were virgins; each was just as clumsy and unsure as the other. They masked their uncertainties and insecurities between the sheets, cloaked in darkness whilst they imitated what they had seen in films, read in books and imagined in their mind's eyes as Jason's inexperienced fingers ineptly slid on a condom.

Her first experience of sex felt uneventful. The delicious ecstasy that women portrayed in so many films was a far cry from the dull stabbing ache she felt inside her.

'Let me go on top,' she instructed Jason.

But it was still the same feeling, only now the uncomfortable ache felt even sharper, almost painful. *Is this it? This isn't what I expected sex to feel like.*

'Babe, something's wrong with the condom! Something's wrong!' Jason shrieked and pushed her off him.

'What's the matter? What's happened?'

'The condom!'

They both stared down at his penis, its uncircumcised head poked out like a latex turtleneck sweater.

'Yup, it's broken.' She inspected, doing her utmost to remain as calm as possible, given how hysterical Jason had become.

'It's . . . it's broken. It's broken! Shit! Fuck!' Jason shrieked. 'Shit. Shit. SHIT!' Jason's head now in his hands.

Great. The first time I ever have sex, and this happens. Perfect. Thoughts to herself as she almost let out a laugh at the absurdity of the whole situation.

'Where are you going?' said Jason, now slightly less hysterical.

'To go check if there's any cum inside me,' she said calmly. Inside she was screaming with panic.

In the shower, piping hot water pounded on her back as she stuck two fingers inside herself. There was nothing there, all clear. Nothing was inside her, not even blood. Jason would later ask her why she didn't bleed.

'I thought girls did that, you know, bleed on their first time . . . It was your first time, right?'

She would later recount the incident when her hymen broke in the middle of the night when she was ten years old. She thought it was her period. What she wouldn't tell him was how her Auntie Yin diapered her up with a huge maxi pad that chafed her thighs when she walked. She didn't tell him that she had to be excused from her P.E. lesson with a note in her school diary with big blue biro letters reading <u>MENSTRUATION</u>. She didn't tell him that she could feel the maxi pad sticking out through her thin blue and white school-uniform dress. Some things were just not meant to be shared with your fifteen-year-old boyfriend.

She got out of the shower and stared at herself in the steamed-up mirror. *You're no longer a virgin. You just had sex. That's it.* Studying herself, she tried to find any signs that something had changed, that something was now different. *Would my mother be able to know I've had sex? Can she tell? Can others tell?* But there was nothing. Nothing was different, she looked exactly the same. Except for the dull ache between her legs, deep inside her, she also felt exactly the same. She didn't know what she should have expected post-sex, but she had certainly expected something a lot more dramatic. *What an anti-climax. Literally. I hope sex is going to get better after this.*

TWENTY

LESSONS IN TOLERANCE

tolerance

/ˈtɒl(ə)r(ə)ns/   *The ability or willingness to tolerate the existence of*

noun   *opinions or behaviour that one dislikes or disagrees with.*

Since she was a little girl, her Paupau taught her that one of the greatest virtues was tolerance. After all, Mr Jesus was more than tolerant of those who persecuted him and eventually crucified him.

'Must live by Mr Jesus example. He tolerant. Must be tolerant,' her Paupau would say.

She thought she understood what tolerance meant. When the girls at her school in Hong Kong joined in with the rugby boys and ridiculed her attempts at being sexy, she swallowed her rage and humiliation. *Tolerance*. When the girls at her new school in Paris sniggered and mocked her cheap clothes as she walked past, she withheld her urge to smash their skulls against the wall. *Tolerance. Must tolerate,* she would remind herself.

But when her eighteen-year-old stepbrother Sebastian pushed a button that she didn't even know she had, she came to learn the true meaning of tolerance and subsequently decided to reject the notion altogether. She was fifteen.

Sebastian was a social-status snob. He had been brought up in an upper-middle class environment that valued manners and social etiquette above all else, respect for other's personal space and boundaries; he simply chose to ignore all of that when it came to the girl and her mother. Had his new stepmother come from old money—perhaps one of those wealthy Hong Kong families that lived on the Peak—he may have afforded her some sort of superficial courtesy. But to Sebastian, his new stepmother and sister were '*asiatiques vulgaires*', and therefore did not deserve his respect. But it wasn't just him. Georges' family disproved of the marriage, assuming her mother was a gold digger and had married Georges just to obtain a French passport. Their disdain for her mother could not be concealed. The girl watched as they sized her mother up and turned up their noses at her cheap clothes and lack of Western decorum. *Fucking racists.*

Sebastian lived in a studio flat that conjoined with the main part of the barge equipped with all his own amenities, but this did not stop him from intruding into the girl's room and helping himself to her en suite bathroom every time he had returned from a long night of partying. It was utterly bizarre.

The first time it happened, the girl was petrified. It was probably around 4 or 5 a.m. and on a school night. Deep in slumber, the girl didn't hear the wooden door slide open. She couldn't hear clumsy intoxicated steps towards her bathroom. Suddenly she awoke when the bath tap was turned on. Her heart thumped out of her chest. *What was that? A loud bang? Was someone in here? Someone is in here! Oh my God!* She opened her eyes but except for the shadows cast by the Parisian lights outside, she could see nothing. She didn't dare move, for she was convinced it was an intruder who had come to rob her, kill her or worse, rape her. She tried to pry her eyes as wide as she could to suck up as much of what she could see as possible. Lying perfectly still and doing all she could not to scream, she waited and prayed to whatever deity that this person would leave as quickly as possible without noticing her. Strange water sounds—someone was taking a bath. *An intruder is taking a bath? In my tub? What the hell?* Twenty minutes later the intruder got out of the tub and left. She waited until she was sure there was complete silence and switched on the lights.

Boxer shorts on the floor. Boxer shorts that she recognised from watching her mother do the laundry. *Eww! Sebastian! What the hell? Yuck!*

The next morning, she reported the incident to her mother, who in turn told Georges. The girl expected her stepfather to be outraged at his son's utter lack of respect for her personal space and privacy. She expected Georges to empathise with how terrified she had been or how unacceptable Sebastian's behaviour was. Instead the girl was stoically assured that it wouldn't happen again and not to worry. She tried to believe them.

But it did happen again. A few weeks later when her stepfather was away on a business trip, Sebastian intruded into the girl's room in the middle of the night and helped himself to her bathroom. This time he went out of his way to make as much noise as he could, banging, slamming, thumping. He had a point to make— *I can do whatever the fuck I want, and you can't do shit.* She wanted to scream at him, lob books at the door, shake him; she wanted to do something. She even imagined drowning him in his own bath water, holding him under by his neck. *Tolerance. Remember, tolerance.* She could hear her Paupau's voice in her head, so she swallowed her anger and did the sensible thing by reporting the incident to her mother who passed it up the chain of command. Words fell on deaf ears as Sebastian continued to openly defy his father's wishes and kept repeating his behaviour. Now Sebastian decided that he would not only barge in whenever he wanted and leave his dirty boxer shorts on her bathroom floor but his aftershave, dirty socks and razor. It was his territory now.

Once the girl came home after a trip away with friends to a used condom in her bed. She felt violated. A complete disregard for her private space. *In my bed?! My fucking bed?! What is wrong with this boy? How can he do something like this?*

She was certain that this time Georges would step up to his responsibility in parenting his son and impose consequences for his disgusting behaviour. She was sure that she could trust the 'man of the household' to handle this ongoing problem they had and protect her from Sebastian. After all, wasn't this why her mother married him, so that a man could protect them?

'I will speak with him about this,' said Georges.

That's it? You will speak to him about this? What? Is this the best that you can do? The girl was astonished at her stepfather's response. The only man she had come to view as a potential 'father figure' was unable to protect her from his own son. Yet again, she was disappointed, only this time it cemented her views about him, about fathers and about men.

Out of respect for the home life that her mother was trying to create, the girl bit her tongue and saved her livid frustration for her mother. As she lashed out, her mother simply nodded along in agreement, knowing there was nothing at that moment that could have calmed the girl down.

'He is so disrespectful! I fucking hate him! He can't do this, Ma! He can't! What's wrong with him? Argh! How can you put up with this?'

'Calm. Calm down! I know, I know. But must be tolerant, okay? Must be tolerant. Everyone needs time to adjust, new lifestyle new family. Takes time. Takes tolerance. Be tolerant,' heeded her mother.

This is bullshit. Tolerance is bullshit. For the sake of her mother, the girl did her best to respect her wishes and suppress her anger. But everyone has a breaking point.

That breaking point happened to be on a particularly hot July afternoon. The girl had just returned home from the library and was giddy at the prospect of watching VHS films whilst drinking ice-cold Coca-Cola. A whole lazy afternoon to herself; there was no better way to escape the humidity. But her giddiness quickly spewed into fury.

With Georges away on yet another business trip, Sebastian decided to take advantage of his absence and invite his friends over to the family home without notifying anyone who actually lived there. Their living room had become a cannabis den. The entire house reeked. The place was a sty: the glass coffee table was littered with weed residue, hashish, discarded rolling papers and filters. A bong, CDs, half-eaten pizza crusts, ash, cigarette butts, empty bottles and cans littered the place. Sticky patches covered the wooden floor. Brown stains from unknown substances marked their Bordeaux-red couch. The TV had been pushed to the other side of the living room, wires all over the place. *C'était un bordel.*

'Ma, have you seen this?' shouted the girl.

The girl marched towards her mother, who stood calmly in their open-plan kitchen as she slapped her marigolds on.

'Yes. I was here.' Her mother made no eye contact.

'And you didn't say anything? Or do anything? Huh?'

'What could I do? They just ignore me.' Her mother sighed as she looked up, eyes full of frustration.

'You could have told them to leave!' The girl couldn't help but raise her voice.

'And you think they leave? You think they listen to me?'

'You could've called the police?!'

'And then what would Georges say?'

'Eh, I don't know, maybe that his son's an asshole?!'

The daughter couldn't recognise her mother, who used to stand on the girl's pedestal of strong, defiant women, who now looked so small. Her mother who stood up for herself and had walloped a woman twice her size across the supermarket with a durian, now voiceless against a spoiled teenage stepson. *Who are you?* She couldn't comprehend nor accept how her mother's backbone could so easily bend for a superficial sense of normality. Nor could she understand how or why her mother could allow this, could tolerate this.

'You don't understand. Some day when you get married you understand. We all must try our best to be a family. Just be tolerant. Be tolerant. Okay?' her mother pleaded.

'But what if I don't want to?' the girl spat out.

Her mother didn't respond. Instead she began to clean the mess Sebastian and his friends had left.

The girl took a deep breath and thought if she could just put on one of her tapes, all would be well, and she would then be able to help her mother clean up this filth. *Just chill and count backwards from ten. All will be fine. Ten, nine, eight, seven, six, five, four, three, three, two . . . two . . . two . . . Fuck this!*

The TV wasn't switching on. The VCR wasn't working either. Sebastian and his friends had moved the TV causing the wires to come undone. This only meant one thing: she wouldn't be able to watch her tapes and enjoy her ice-cold Coca-Cola. He had fucked up her afternoon plans. The girl was very meticulous, to the point of being anal about sticking to her plans. *That's it! FUCK THIS! FUCK HIM!*

The girl picked up his bong and slammed it on the glass coffee table, and the bong shattered. Her mother dashed towards her.

'What happened? What is going on? What are you doing?' shrieked her mother.

But the girl was too enraged to respond. She charged into the kitchen, grabbed a black bin bag and marched into her bathroom, chucked all of Sebastian's belongings into the bag, opened the window and threw it out. Luckily for her they lived on a barge and his belongings merely sank to the bottom of the Seine.

She wasn't done. Her frenzy fuelled her further as she went for the CDs that he had left on the coffee table. One by one she opened up the case, took the CDs out and snapped them into pieces. *Fucking asshole. I hate you. You fuck.* It felt therapeutically liberating.

'Stop! Stop! You'll cut yourself!'

Her mother was taken aback by the girl's cold and focussed wrath. She had never seen her daughter so unresponsive. When the last CD was broken, she put all the pieces in a bag, wrote on a piece of paper 'NEXT TIME CLEAN UP

AFTER YOURSELF!', walked out and placed the bag outside Sebastian's door.

A few hours passed. The girl had been waiting for Sebastian's return the whole time with a huge knot in her stomach—an anxious knot. She could feel something big was going to happen, she just wasn't sure what. When Sebastian came in, he went straight to the house phone. Given his lack of response, she assumed he had not yet seen his bag of surprise, so she decided to take action.

'*La télévision ne marche pas.* The TV, it's not working,' she hollered at him.

No response.

'SEBASTIAN, *je te parle*! I'm talking to YOU! I said, the TV's not working.'

'Good for you.'

'What? What d'you say? You broke the TV. You fucking fix it!'

Sebastian slammed the phone down and marched up to her. The girl stood up from the sofa. She was ready. Whatever he was going to give her, she was ready for it. *Come at me, I'm ready.*

'What did you fucking say to me?' he hissed at her.

'You broke the TV. You must fix it.'

'Fuck you, *salope*.'

'Fuck me? Fuck you, *pute*.'

The girl's chest pumped out, poking her finger at him, eyes glaring.

'D'you even know who I am? You speak to me like that?'

He got right up in her face, his words spitting out at her. He was more than a head taller than her, but she wasn't prepared to back down. Not now, not ever—he had to learn.

'I don't give a shit. You're a fucking asshole. *Connard. Pute*!'

'You fucking bitch!'

Sebastian raised his fist to strike her, but before he could even land the strike, the girl's mother pounced on him like a tiger protecting her cub and pinned him right against the wall. Lightning speed, thunder strength.

'Now you listen to me, you son of a bitch! You raise even just one finger on my daughter, I cut your fucking balls off!' her mother roared.

For a split-second Sebastian was motionless. He couldn't believe how this tiny Hong Kongese pushover could become a monster ready to eat him. They began to shove at each other and grapple. Instinct struck the girl. Terrified Sebastian would strike her mother or throw her to the ground, she ran into the kitchen and pulled out the biggest knife she could find and pointed it at him.

'Get away from my mother, you fucking asshole!' the girl snarled at him.

Knife in hand, she was ready to plunge the blade into his flesh. Sebastian's face instantly turned white. Both his hands jumped up as he slowly tiptoed backwards.

'PUT THE KNIFE DOWN!' shouted her mother.

'I could fucking kill you, you fucking asshole! You have no clue who I am. No clue!' the girl barked and snarled at Sebastian, who was now trembling.

'PLEASE PUT THE KNIFE DOWN! NOW! DO IT!' Again, her mother pleaded.

'I-I . . . I'm so-rr-yyy.' Sebastian's face was humbled by tears.

'You fucking come near me or my mother ever again, you'll be sorry.'

'PUT IT DOWN, PLEASE. PUT IT DOWN!' beseeched her mother.

As soon as the girl lowered her hand, Sebastian sprinted out of there. She could hear him crying all the way out. Her mother slowly crept towards the girl and took her by the wrist to disarm her. The moment the girl caught her mother's eye, she let out a big cry. She was so fed up. Fed up of having to be 'tolerant', of having to put up with Sebastian, of having to watch him and Georges' other children disrespect her mother, of having to bite her tongue or restrain her fists whenever Georges' friends or relatives would make sly racist snobby remarks about her mother. Fed up. She wasn't going to tolerate this any more. No more.

The girl never got to watch her tapes nor drink her Coca-Cola that afternoon, but it didn't matter because from that day forward Sebastian stopped using her bathroom, stopped bringing his friends over for his parties, stopped leaving used condoms in her bed and stopped speaking to her mother disrespectfully. In fact, he stopped any contact altogether. She learnt what the true meaning of tolerance was that afternoon. Tolerance meant keeping your mouth shut even when someone disrespected you or family. Tolerance meant biting your tongue even though your personal space was being violated. Tolerance meant hiding your disappointment at the people you had entrusted to protect you. Tolerance meant silence. No, the girl hated that word and she still does to this day. *Fuck tolerance.*

TWENTY-ONE

LAP IT UP

She had heard the saying that you never forget your first, but she was never warned about what happens when your 'first' dumps you out of the blue and in the most tortuous of ways. She wished someone had told her, even instructed her, on how to navigate the turbine of shit flung post-breakup. Would that have changed anything? Would she have listened?

Mid-August. Her first complete summer in Paris. Life had finally begun to settle. Sebastian had just learnt his lesson about the girl's level of tolerance, and it was only two weeks until her boyfriend Jason would return from the U.S. Sixteen days to be exact. The girl had been counting down the days with Post-It notes in nervous anticipation for her boyfriend to come back and for them to start Year Eleven at school together.

Four weeks of ten-page handwritten letters back and forth, expensive international phone calls interrupted by parental reminders of the cost and gentle strolls to the nearby American Library to use their internet email service. This went on throughout July.

Then something changed, something had happened. First, the phone calls stopped. *Well, I guess those calls were really expensive. Long distance costs a lot.* Then the emails stopped. *Well, I guess he's just really busy.* Then the letters stopped. *Well, I guess . . . I guess . . . I don't know.*

Her letters had no replies. Whenever she called Jason, there was always some excuse as to why he couldn't come to the phone. *Something is very wrong. This isn't like Jason at all.* She felt it in her gut, she just had no idea what it was nor what would transpire.

Then one day, she finally received an odd letter from Jason. Giddy with excitement, she clutched the envelope in her hand, but the letter felt uncharacteristically thin. She tore it open. On a single sheet, it read:

WHEN I GET BACK, WE NEED TO TALK.

x J

There was nothing else, just that single sentence. *That can't be right.* She flipped over the letter hoping there would be more written on the other side but there was nothing. *That can't be right.* So, she went back to the letterbox in search for another letter. Nothing. A lump in her throat began to form as her guts twisted up. *There's gotta be an explanation. I'll just talk to Jason and everything will be okay. But what if he doesn't come back? What if he decides he wants to stay in the States? No, that can't be it. There's some kind of misunderstanding,* she told herself as her shaking finger punched his number into the phone.

'Hello? Yes. Hello, can I speak with Jason, please?'

'One second. J! Phone!'

It was his mother. His mother always liked the girl. Long pause. Muffled voices. More pause.

'Yeah?'

'Jason! Hi! It's me.'

'Yeah.'

'Umm. I got your last letter . . . you said you needed to talk? Is everything okay?'

'Yeah . . . when I get back . . . I don't want to do this now.'

His voice once so in love and hungry to speak with her for hours until their ears went numb, sounded unusually distracted and standoffish.

'Jason, is everything okay? You sound . . . well . . . different.'

'No. Everything's fine. We'll talk when I get back. Okay? I gotta go.'

CLICK. The girl was caught off guard. Conversations that used to end with a play-fight as to who should hang up first and how many 'I love yous' could be said, now reduced to the sound of the phone beeping.

The girl looked at the Post-It note countdown. *Sixteen days. Sixteen days and all will be fine. Jason just needs to see you, and everything will be fine. Right?* The wait over the next two weeks was brutal on her guts as she waited anxiously, anticipating for day zero to come.

Day zero arrived. She waited. She waited by the phone all dolled up and ready to be beckoned by her Jason. She waited for him to call, for him to tell her he had arrived home, for him to tell her to come over, for them to have their magical romantic reunion. She waited. Noon. No call. 2 p.m. Still no call. 4 p.m. Nothing. The girl grew impatient and restless. *I'll just go there and wait for him at his place then. I've got to see him. This isn't like him at all. I'm sure everything will be okay.*

The twenty-minute walk from her barge across Bir Hakeim bridge into Passy—Paris' swanky arrondissement home to some of the city's wealthiest residents—felt like the longest walk she had ever taken. She was excited to see Jason, but each step fuelled her anxiety. *Why do I feel like something isn't quite right?*

Jittery hands inserted a copy of the key he had left her into his maroon front door. Loud death metal music pounding through. *That's weird. Jason hates death metal. Is someone home already?*

Just as the girl was about to turn the key, the door flew open. There he was—her Jason, all 6 ft 2 inches of him.

'Hi babe! I've missed you so much!'

With both arms she reached over to embrace her tall lover, but he just stood there motionless like a tree. She tip-toed, reaching to try to kiss him. Flinch.

'Why d'you use my key?'

'Eh . . . what? What d'you mean? You gave it to me so I could come over when I wanted to.'

'Well, give it back to me.' He didn't even look at her.

'J, what's going on? Why do you suddenly want your key back? You said we needed to talk? Can we talk?'

She followed him into his room and was startled to see Rob, his best friend, at Jason's desk.

'Oh. Hey, Rob. J, I didn't think we were having company? What's going on?'

Her eyes moved past Jason's desk and she got her answer. The gold photo frame that used to house a photo of them embracing in Disneyland Paris was now replaced with a semi-nude autographed photo of Cameron Diaz. The glass cabinet door that used to be adorned with collages of photos of her and them had been ripped off and now lay pathetically on the floor. They were all replaced by pictures of Christina and Britney.

'What happened to you?' Her voice quivered. *Do not cry. He cannot see you cry.*

'Nothing. Well . . . I guess some things . . . HA! HA! HA!' forced laughter.

'What happened? What is this? What's going on?'

She was trying to search for an answer in his eyes, but he couldn't even look at her.

'Nothing's going on. People change, okay? You change. I change.'

'Look at me, J. LOOK at me. Can we at least talk about this?'

'Yeah, sure. Let's talk.' She sat on his sofa bed as she watched Jason grab a VHS and stick it in his VCR.

'Hey, Rob, did I ever tell you she's dynamite at giving head? She'll suck your cock right off,' Jason bragged loudly.

Words taken from her worst American jock nightmare. Words she would never imagine he would utter.

'What the fuck, J?' Repulsed, she stood up to grab her bag. 'What the fuck's wrong with you?'

'Hey, before you go, you gotta see this. Just have a look at the TV.'

Jason switched on the TV. Big veiny cock fucking a gagging mouth attached to blown-up silicone lips. Big cock choking this woman until it emerged and sprayed all over her face. Faceless hands grabbed her by her hair, pushing her face into his cum.

'Lap it up. It's right. Lap it up! HA! HA! HA!' Jason's words as he belted out loud forced laughs.

Rob looked at the girl and shrugged, as if to say he too could not comprehend Jason's abnormal change of behaviour.

'She's almost as good as you! HA! HA! HA! Let's watch it again, shall we?' More forced laughter.

The girl ran out of there as fast as she could, sobbing all the way home.

That night she waited until she knew Rob would have gone home and she phoned Jason. After over ten unanswered calls, he finally picked up.

'I don't understand . . . How can you just suddenly change like this? What happened?'

'I dunno, I guess I just did. You've changed, so I changed.'

'What? What are you talking about? I didn't change. I've been waiting for you to come back all summer. Don't you love me any more?' She couldn't believe what was happening. She suddenly felt like she was no longer attached to her body, that she had somehow drifted up to the ceiling and was looking down at herself. *Why won't he answer me? Come on, say something. Please. Just say something.*

There was no answer. The girl broke her own promise as she began to cry.

'J, you still love me, right? . . . I love you so much. How . . . I mean . . . how? What happened? I don't understand. What is happening? What did I do?'

There was still no answer. All she could hear between her weeps was his breathing.

'Answer me. Please! ANSWER ME!' she begged and screamed.

'I still love you . . . I just don't want to be with you any more.'

'But why? I don't understand. You need to tell me. Why?' The girl searched her memories trying to think of something, anything that Jason could construe as a valid reason for dumping her. *What could I have possibly done that would deserve this?*

'You know. You know what you did.'

CLICK.

What is going on? How did this happen? What does Jason think I have done? Why won't he tell me? This can't be happening!

She had wished for a lot of things throughout her fifteen years in this life but in that moment, she wanted to retract all those wishes in exchange for just a single wish. Just one. She wished that someone had told her or even warned her about this moment: the moment she felt her heart was being carved out by a blunt spoon. Scraped out like rotten fruit, teaspoon by teaspoon, until there was nothing there, just hollowed pain.

Six years passed. The girl learnt with the passage of time how to heal, to move on and that there would be many more torturous and painful moments to come.

When she had almost forgotten about the scar tissue that Jason had left inside her, one day out of the blue, Jason found her on Facebook and messaged her. After a few messages back and forth, they were soon scheduling phone calls to accommodate their time zones. Phone calls that swallowed hours as they reminisced their first love. Nostalgia can be beautiful until you unlock too many rooms in your memory palace.

'Jason, I need to ask you something . . . It's been bothering me for a long, long time.'

'Yeah, sure! You can ask me anything.'

'Why did you break up with me? You never actually told me.'

'I'm pretty sure I did . . . Didn't I?'

'No. You didn't. Remember, you came back from the U.S. that summer, and you just decided you didn't want to be with me any more, remember?'

'Oh.' Slight pause. 'Yeah. Erh, I guess you're right. I guess I never did. But . . . you know why.'

'Know why what?'

'Really, you don't remember? You cheated. You cheated on me with Sultan.'

'What? What you talking about? I never cheated.'

'Yeah, you did. You cheated on me with Sultan. Aisha said—'

'Wait, what? Aisha said what? That's bullshit. That never happened!'

'Well, she said—'

'And you just believed her? Just like that? You never thought to ask me? Maybe confront me about it? Or try to find out if it was even true?'

'Well . . . I mean, it was . . . I mean you did, didn't you?'

'No! I swear, I've never cheated on you. Why would I?'

'Shit . . . that's bad. I mean I just assumed 'cause Aisha said you guys had a "thing" and then I saw you two together outside school one day—'

'What day? When?'

'You know that day . . . it was raining. You were waiting for me to finish class. I saw you. I saw you with Sultan. You were wearing his jacket.'

'Oh! That day. Come on, J, nothing happened. It was raining and I was really cold waiting outside on the bench for you. Sultan walked past, saw I was cold, gave me his jacket and a smoke. Plus, we were in public!'

'He had a thing for you.'

'Yeah, I know. But we never did anything.'

'Well, yeah, but you guys would go off and have a smoke and then that summer Aisha called. She said you and Sultan were fucking.'

The girl took a deep breath.

'Well, you could've at least asked me if it was true or at least told me why you broke up with me. That shit took me a long time to get over.'

'I know. But it didn't go down well considering you and Sultan did end up together a couple months after.'

A long pause.

'Well, shit happens.'

'Hey, can you imagine if Aisha never said those things and that we didn't break up? And then you never got with Sultan after?' As soon as he posed that question, her mind transported her to his room. Porn on the TV glaring back at her and his voice jeering: *Lap it up. Lap it up.*

'Yeah. Just imagine.'

SWALLOW YOU WHOLE

I wanted you so
badly that I wrote
Your name hundreds of times
On lined A4 paper
And tore you up.
In my frenzy I stuffed
You into my mouth
And chewed upon you
As you sliced tiny paper
Cuts along the inside
Of my mouth.
I chewed and chewed
Until you became a soggy mess.
No one told me
I didn't have to swallow.

TWENTY-TWO

BIG PROBLEM

'Hello?'

She hoped it would be Jason, calling her to tell her their breakup had all been a sick prank or a crushing nightmare and that everything could go back to normal. But it wasn't.

'Hey!'

An unfamiliar voice instead on the other side. Thick Nigerian accent whom she couldn't quite place. Who had she given her number to?

'Um, who's this?'

'Can't you tell who it is by my voice? Baby, you've hurt my feelings now.'

She paused for a moment, confused why someone she didn't know would call her.

'Erh, who is this?'

'It's Patrick, baby.'

'Oh. How did you even get my number?'

'Devanshi, she gave it to me.'

'Oh.'

'You don't sound too pleased about that.'

'Well . . . I'm just . . . surprised.'

No. She wasn't surprised, not at all. Thanks to Jason's unsolicited anecdotes about their sex life when they were together, rumours had spread around school, drawing unwanted attention from pesky hormone-driven boys—boys like Patrick who lingered around her like a bad smell that just won't go away.

'So, Patrick. What's up?'

'I thought you could help me out.'

'Erh. Okay . . .'

'You're just so . . . damn fine, girl. You're one fine piece of ass. And you see, it's giving me a big problem.'

'Um, okay. Erh, thank you . . . I guess? Is that all? 'Cause I have to go now.'

She should have hung up. She should have ended the conversation right there and then. She should have reminded herself that following social conventions to be civil, to be polite, to go along with it, was a big pile of bullshit. But she didn't. She stayed on the phone.

'Hey! Wait a sec. Don't go. Like I said, I have this big, big problem.'

Heavy breaths coming from the other end. Muffled voice.

'Umm, Patrick? What, erh . . . what's that sound?'

The thought of what it could be repulsed her. Immediately she shoved the image to the far corners of her mind.

'I think you know what's that sound, baby. You know you like it.'

Heavier breathing. Tapping, tugging sounds in the background. Tap. Tap. Tap. Tug. Tug. Tug.

'I'm hanging up now.'

'No. Don't go. Tell me, what colour panties you got on and are they wet?'

'Eww. Fuck off!'

She immediately slammed the phone down and kicked it under her bed. Hugging her knees, she shuddered in revulsion on the floor. For hours she tried desperately to shake off the sordid images of Patrick on the other end of the line, with his hand around his cock, jerking off to her. When she finally stood up, she disconnected her phone and shoved it into her desk drawer.

Even in my own fucking room. You've got to get to me even in my own room. Intruded upon. Trespassed. Invaded. Defiled. Violated. Fuck off.

TWENTY-THREE

HEY, FOXY. HEY, LUCA

'Hey Foxy.' Big Cheshire cat smile. Always the same delicious smile, always the same greeting.

'Hey Luca.'

'Come on in.'

Lucas, or Luca as they knew and called him, had become the girl's most trusted ally and smoking buddy since the start of Year Eleven. Luca, a sixteen-year-old Argentine with warm olive skin and thick silky black hair. What he lacked in broad shoulders and bulging biceps, Luca more than compensated for in his intoxicating charm, his family's aristocratic wealth and his suave generosity. Whilst his American peers rolled into school with their oversized tattered jeans and unkempt hair, Luca strolled in in a Ralph Lauren suit, polished brogues and an Hermès belt. He had a style unmatched by the Neanderthals of their international school. He was a beautiful boy.

Luca came from a wealth she had never seen before. Their family owned a three-storey mansion just off the Champs-Élysées. The first time she was brought to Luca's home, she tried to conceal her astonishment. *What the hell do your parents do? Diplomats? Drug dealers? Lottery ticket winners? What the fuck? You guys have a lift in your home? Your own lift? And you have the top floor to yourself? What the fuck? Who are you?* Just a few thoughts as she brushed past the full-size pool table in their rec room.

Once she had asked Luca whom he lived with because she never saw anyone apart from his cleaner in the whole building.

'My Mum, she lives here. I don't see her much. And my older brother too. And Juanita, my housekeeper. Actually, are you hungry? I can ask Juanita to fix you something?'

'Nah, that's okay. Um, Luca, do you ever get lonely?'

'Lonely? No, not at all. Why?' He laughed.

'Because you're in this huge home, usually by yourself.'

'That's why I always have people over. So, I won't have to be.'

'Alone?'

'No, lonely.'

Luca was seldomly so open with anyone. The girl would later learn that his extrovert charisma was merely a mask that he wore around his peers.

The first time the girl paid a private visit to Luca's, she had already been seeing Sultan for a couple of months.

Hey Foxy. How r u? Come over.

She read and re-read Luca's text message. That's odd, a direct message to her.

Sultan's w Mo.

She texted back. She had assumed he was trying to reach Sultan and decided to reach him through her.

I no. Come over. Want 2 C U.

Y?

Need ur Zippo.

OK. 20 min.

Quick wardrobe change, makeup check and perfume dousing, Zippo in pocket, she marched up the Champs-Élysées. Even though she had lived in Paris for over a year, the magnificent beauty of the Champs never failed to take her breath away. It was handy that Luca lived a mere twenty-minute walk from her home—the close proximity would later make visiting her ally a treasured comfort.

Six hours melted away and they were still hotboxed in his studio. She had never been so stoned. Her eyes stung from the smoke, blood-vessel red. Cotton mouth, limbs draped on his sofa. Muted MTV as Buddha-Bar lounge music played in the background. His head nestled on her lap, blowing smoke into her mouth.

'Hey Foxy.'

Big Cheshire cat smile. Barely opened eyelids looking up at her.

'This is the beginning of a very bizarre friendship, Luca,' she muttered to him. He just smiled in response.

TWENTY-FOUR

SUPERPOWERS

She had always wanted a superpower. Telepathy, telekinesis, control over the weather, ability to predict the future, eyes that shot lightning, awesome fighting skills—any of those would have been fantastically brilliant. But no, superheroes never seem to be able to choose their powers. She was, without her consent, bestowed with invisibility.

In a room full of teenage boys, waving their dicks around along with their overinflated egos and tribal talk of tits and ass, it was hard to be the only vagina in the room. Harder still to be the only visible and audible vagina in the room. Much harder when those boys had been chugging beers and toking blunts all night before heading to an after-hours snooker room. She had tagged along as Sultan's girlfriend and earned her place as a 'cool chick', whatever 'cool chick' was supposed to mean. It seemed to mean that she was invisible.

They were all playing pool, most of them terribly. The combination of booze and cannabis did not aid their hand-eye coordination. First hour passed, and then the next . . . and then the next. During that time, it occurred to her that everyone had asked everyone else to play, even the worst player amongst them, except her. No one asked if she wanted to join in and had she not have been so stoned, she would have probably asked to play. She was awful at snooker but they didn't know that. They had completely bypassed the idea of a girl playing against one of them, because girls don't count; vaginas are no competition.

It wasn't done maliciously nor even intentionally; it simply never occurred to them that a female would and could count.

A female definitely didn't count a few weeks later when they all hotboxed themselves into Luca's studio and decided to prove their masculinity through the ultimate test—the arm-wrestle. She thought there was something very odd and yet endearing in that; their status in the teenage-boy-tribe was their ability to physically overpower the other. *Why don't they just bare-knuckle fight right here? It'll certainly be a lot more entertaining than watching these losers with their lanky arms try and prove something.*

'I want a go,' the girl puckered up.

No response. Perhaps they didn't hear her. So, she spoke louder: 'Let me try. I want a go.'

They all stopped and looked at her, perplexed at her request.

'You serious? Nah . . . Come on!' brushed off one of them.

'No way, you're a girl. It won't be fair,' said another.

'He's right. It won't be fair, it wouldn't be right,' said someone else.

'No. I want a go. Just let me try,' she insisted.

'Fine. Mark, you go first,' said Luca as he pushed Mark towards the girl.

Mark. Stocky fifteen-year-old Egyptian boy. Small feet. 'This'll be easy. Don't say I didn't warn you.' He smirked at her as the others jeered.

But it wasn't so easy for Mark. She took him down without much of a fight. Big roaring chortles. The boys couldn't contain themselves.

'Mark! What the fuck, man? You got your ass handed to you by a girl!' chuckled one of them.

'Fuck man. She's strong! You don't believe me? You try!' shouted Mark, eyes wide open in disbelief.

One of them, Boe, stood up and sat opposite her. His grey eyes stained red from the smoke.

'I'll take it easy on you, baby.' He winked.

It was cute. It was sweet, but what was sweeter was watching Boe's hand touch the table and the thunder of laughs from her small audience.

'Fuck! Fuck!' jolted Boe, eyes darting towards Mark as if to share some kind of defeatist solidarity.

'What the fuck, Boe? I thought the Dutch were strong?' teased Luca.

Luca was in hysterics but not the others. The others were still in shock with their swollen egos damaged. The girl savoured the moment. She was being seen . . . finally. Not for the ass and tits, not for being 'Sultan's girl', not for being the 'cool chick' that tagged along. No. For the first time, she knew they saw her as possibly an equal.

'Hold up!' piped up Sultan as he kissed his teeth. 'She's not that strong. You guys . . . we've been smoking all night. That shit's gonna make us limp. She only beat you guys 'cause she hasn't smoked as much as y'all.'

Sultan, her own boyfriend. In one fell swoop he had thrown her under the bus in order to save them face. The split second of respect she just gained amongst them was all gone. It was taken from her by her own boyfriend, simply because they couldn't handle losing to a girl.

'Oh yeah. That's right, man! Ha! And I thought she was that strong,' added Mark.

'You're lucky, Sweet Face,' said Boe.

Their smirks were back, and she was back to being invisible again. *Stupid fucking superpower.*

TWENTY-FIVE

NO GREATER RUSH

Tuesday. As soon as her end-of-term exams finished that morning, the girl dragged her best gal pal Sophia to Châtelet—home to an eclectic mix of vintage and goth shops, independent brands, artists, and some unsavoury characters. They had to kill several hours in McDonald's whilst they waited for the tattoo parlours to open. After a few dubious hygiene standards and a couple of unsuccessful attempts, she landed upon American Body Art Tattoo Parlour.

'Can I help you?'

'Yeah, I would like to get a tattoo. Today, please,' the girl said nervously.

'Huh,' said the man, eyeballing her up and down.

He was heavily decorated with patterns and colours, adorned with metal in every orifice. She had never seen anything like it up close, and the sight of him unnerved her. *I hope it's not going to be him that tattoos me . . .*

'You wanna get tattooed? Today?'

'Yes. Today, please.'

The girl stood tall as she wondered how older people usually behave. *Just act normal. Keep your shit together or he'll ID you.* She gave her best impression of an adult and looked at the man straight in the eyes, refusing to break her gaze.

'Okay. Pick a design from the folders,' he said as he waved her away.

The girl exhaled. *Don't lose your cool yet. He can still ID you and kick you out.* Trying to act nonchalant, the girl flicked through the folders until her eyes landed on the visual representation of the tattoo she wanted. *Yes, that's the one! That one.*

'Erh, excuse me . . . I want this one, please,' she said pointing to her desired design.

'Okay.'

'How much will that cost?'

'Six hundred francs.' This was the equivalent to £80.

'Oh . . . Erm, I only have five hundred, cash.' She had spent six months saving this sum.

She pulled out her cash from her purse as proof.

'Okay,' he agreed and eyeballed her up and down again. 'Five hundred. Come back in an hour.'

As soon as the girl stepped outside where her friend Sophia had been waiting, they screamed with excitement.

'Your first tattoo! How exciting!' Sophia cheered. She was almost as thrilled as she was.

'I know! I feel like such a rebel! What should we do now? We've got an hour.'

'Let's go get a coffee to kill some time.'

Sophia linked to the girl's arm as they headed to a nearby brassiere.

If only someone had warned the girl that drinking too much coffee before your first tattoo was a terrible idea. With five minutes to go before her appointment, the girl was pacing up and down the pavement outside the parlour, barely able to keep her cigarette steady between her fingers. She had a serious case of the jitters.

'Hey, you okay?' said a man's voice.

She looked up and saw that a middle-aged Rastafarian had stopped in front of her, joint in hand and smile across his face.

'Yeah, just really nervous.'

'Yeah? What you nervous about?'

'Getting my first tattoo.'

'Ah, I see.' Big grin on his face. 'Smoke this.'

He handed over his joint. She took a whiff, looked at him again and breathed smoke.

'Don't rush it, girl, take your time. Relax.'

'I gotta go. It's time for my appointment now. Thanks, man.'

After handing over the five hundred francs, she followed her tattooist, the man who had come outside earlier, down the stairs to a private booth. *Thank God it's not the same guy as before. This guy's a lot less scary looking and actually quite fit.*

'Okay, so where is this going?' the tattooist asked her as he slapped on a fresh pair of latex gloves.

'Um, right here.'

She pulled the waistline of her trousers down and pointed to her coccyx area.

'I want my trousers to be able to cover it.'

'Okay, no problem. Take off your trousers and sit down facing the chair.'

She had never taken her trousers off in front of man that wasn't her boyfriend before. So, when she took off her bottoms and sat cowgirl style on the clingfilm wrapped leather chair, she began to question whether the combination of being stoned, over-caffeinated, anxious and bottomless in front of a stranger was such a great idea. But when you're fifteen and getting your first tattoo instead of being at school or at the library studying for your final exams the next day, there is no greater rush.

Many people would later ask her what getting a tattoo felt like. To this day she struggles with finding the right words to describe the sensation accurately. It depends on where it is on the body. But in that moment, chair between her legs and a man behind her with an electrified needle that makes the same sound as a drill from the dentist, there was no greater pain. No one told her that getting a tattoo on one's spine and so close to the coccyx would be so excruciating. She wished someone had warned her. But who could? None of her friends had tattoos and she had no older siblings.

Her skin was on fire as heat pulsated through her body. She felt her spine tremble with electricity. Gripping onto the top of the chair until her knuckles turned white, she wanted to cry out. *The pain, the delicious pain.*

'Yes. Yes. I know, it hurts. Almost finished.'

Her tattooist tried his best to comfort her, but she struggled to make out his words through the buzzing drilling sounds. She was sweating. Tunnel vision began to take over.

'This area—for your first tattoo? Yeah, super painful. But we're almost there,' he comforted her.

After what felt like hours, he finally announced, 'Okay. All done. Next time, don't smoke beforehand, okay?' He winked at her as he cling-filmed her up and set her on her way.

How did he know? Are my eyes that bloodshot? Oops.

THINGS YOU NEED TO KNOW BEFORE GETTING A TATTOO:
- Don't drink coffee
- Don't get stoned
- Don't pick painful places
- And finally, when you've got one, you'll want more.

TWENTY-SIX

IMPERSONAL PISTOL WHIP

'Let me show you something.'

Sultan grabbed her by the wrist and led her out of his bedroom.

'What? Where are we going?'

'Follow me,' he said as he led them to his father's room and went in.

'But this is your dad's room.'

She stood by the door, every part of her feeling invasive and wrong.

'Yeah, don't worry about it, just close the door. Come.'

Sheepishly she tiptoed into his father's room. She felt as though she were violating some unwritten rule, a rule she had always followed that parents' rooms are no-go areas. But there she was, with Sultan, her Emirati boyfriend of almost six months, standing next to his father's bed, fearful of touching anything. She didn't even want to breathe in there.

Sultan reached above the wardrobe, brought down a black leather briefcase and placed it on the bed. Worn-out edges with frayed stitching. He started to finger a combination, and with the familiar clicking sound, the case popped open. She had never looked inside a man's briefcase before and wasn't quite sure what to expect. As Sultan rummaged carefully through the case, she spotted a couple of passports, folded documents, letters written in Arabic, French, English. *So that's what a man keeps in a briefcase locked up. Huh.*

'It's here somewhere . . . I know it's here . . . Ah! Got it!'

Sultan pulled something out from the piles of documents. There it was, a pistol, black and shiny. She didn't know anything about pistols, only the stuff she had seen in films. She didn't know what kind of pistol it was except it wasn't a revolver, perhaps a 9mm Glock. Big gulp. Her eyes transfixed onto it. She had never seen a pistol before and wasn't sure how to react nor what to feel.

'What the fuck? Is it real?'

She didn't know why she had asked that. *Yes, Sultan's father carries a BB gun with him for shits and giggles, come on!* Then again, she wondered why his father, a diplomat, would have the need for a real handgun.

'Yup. It's real.'

He placed it in his large olive-skinned hand, holding it up for her to see.

'How do you know?' she asked.

Almost immediately there was a click and the magazine popped out. Bronze coloured bullets exposed. Shiny and lethal. Magazine clicked back in.

'Real enough for you?' he asked, smirking at the girl. 'Do you want to touch it?'

Sultan gestured the handgun to her. She stared at the pistol; it was hypnotic. This hand-sized piece of metal with its even smaller little *accoutrements* that can do so much damage. She wondered why she wasn't remotely afraid. She was surprised by how she felt—neither dread nor intrigue. She seemed to feel nothing.

'So? You want to touch it or not?' Sultan was almost giddy. It irritated her.

'It's not a cock, Sultan. No, I don't want to touch it.'

'Oh . . . Okay.'

He was vexed. Sultan had assumed that somehow waving a phallic metal weapon of death would earn him macho points or even turn her on, but it didn't.

'Awww, Sweets, you afraid of the little gun? Aww, don't worry, babe. It's okay. There's nothing to be afraid of. Look, I'll put it away, okay?'

As he patronised her, Sultan placed the pistol back into his father's briefcase. *Yes, that is exactly what it was, Sultan,* she thought to herself, amazed that he had equated her lack of interest with fear. This disappointed her—Sultan had felt the need to patronise her, assuming she would be 'afraid'. But she wasn't afraid, she just didn't give a shit.

After being initially baffled that a diplomat kept a handgun at home, she couldn't care less. In her mind, guns were too easy. They lacked intimacy. They lacked a sort of engagement with the other person. The time it takes between squeezing the trigger and creating perforated bullet-art on a person is minimal. Bang, bang, bang, and that's it. It's done. No, not for her. She had always imagined that if she were ever to commit to taking a human life, she wouldn't bother with a handgun or any firearm for that matter. No, it needed to be intimate, like sex. It would need to be up close and personal, so that she could smell their sweat, their breath, their blood, feel their warmth, to enter into a violent dance for survival. You don't get that with a pistol; it's impersonal. Weapon of choice? Probably a hammer, maybe an axe.

Just before he was about to close the briefcase, he reached in one of the smaller compartments and pulled out an inch-thick wad of five hundred Euro notes. Her eyebrow raised. She was stunned, for she had never seen so much money all at once in front of her before.

'My dad's a proper G! Check it out!'

His eyes glistened as he licked his lips. She had never seen him so excited. Leave it to him to be that turned on by money.

'I think you should put it back. It's not yours. You didn't earn it, Sultan.'

'What? Come on! He's got a whole stash. It's not like he'll miss a note or two.'

With that he pulled out a couple of notes and stashed them into his pocket. Like a criminal, he cleaned up his crime scene.

'People that keep stashes are people who know how to count them. You're spending money that wasn't given to you, that you didn't earn.'

He kissed his teeth at her and pushed her out of his dad's bedroom.

'Don't trip, Sweets. Now let's go have some fun,' he said, disregarding her concern.

That evening her dinner tasted like ash.

That was the first time she saw a pistol. The second time was when Sultan dragged her to Trocadero on an August afternoon just before she was going to leave for boarding school in Cumbria.

The girl didn't particularly want to move to Cumbria, and she couldn't imagine any fifteen-year-old teenage girl would volunteer to live in the middle of nowhere, but the girl felt that she had little choice. Her relationship with her mother had turned turbulent as her mother had to face up to the reality of her daughter's not-so-innocent social life—one of smoking, getting stoned, drinking and being sexually active. More importantly, the girl's French-American International School offered only a very limited choice for A level options, which the girl felt would hinder her chances of entering a top London university.

'I need to go to a school that offers Religious Studies or Philosophy at A level. Or at least better subjects. I'm not going to be able to get the grades I need at this school,' she explained to her mother.

So her mother agreed. But no one had anticipated boarding school fees would be so extortionate. *Are these figures correct? This is in British pounds? Am I seeing this right?* Even the girl thought the fees were excessive and felt guilty that her education was so costly. Luckily, they had managed to locate a state boarding school through the help of the British Consulate who would accept the girl into their sixth-form. *I guess I better make the most of the rest of my time in Paris.*

The afternoon was hot and humid, so much so that her silk skirt clung onto her thighs. They had gone to pick up some weed from Sultan's dealer. This dealer looked like a stereotypical *racaille* with his tilted cap, Lacoste tracksuit bottoms and socks over them. And in typical *racaille* fashion, an Adidas crossbody bag for all his goodies. As he opened his goodie bag, she saw <u>it</u>, right there at the bottom. The long black shiny edge of a pistol. Mr Racaille caught her catching the sight of it and grinned.

'You like it?' he smirked, gesturing to the metal as he licked his lips.

'Is it real?' she blurted.

'Of course, it's real!' Sultan interceded, as he pushed the girl aside, somehow feeling the need to excuse her naivety.

Mr Racaille didn't answer straight away.

'Yes. Yes, it is,' he said, staring at the girl.

'Have you ever used it before?' the girl asked.

He looked at her, then at Sultan and then at the girl again. She didn't flinch as she stared him down. Sultan was incensed by the girl's stupid confidence.

'What are you, the fucking Feds or something? What's with all your questions?' Sultan barked at her.

She didn't like being disciplined by her boyfriend as though she were a child. She didn't like being spoken for, but one thing she instinctively knew was to never argue with your boyfriend in front of another man, so she didn't reply.

'It's cool. She's just curious, let her be curious. Have you ever used one before?'

'No . . . Not really into them. I don't like guns.'

'She's just afraid of them. You know what chicks are like, right?' Sultan again interrupted as he slapped on a superficial smile to conceal his embarrassment. The girl could almost read her boyfriend's mind as if to say, 'Shut the fuck up, you're speaking out of turn.'

'No? Don't like them? Why not?' asked Mr Racaille.

'It's, erm . . . it's impersonal.'

'What? What the fuck are you talking about? Impersonal?! Girl, you be tripping,' Sultan kissed his teeth. 'I'm sorry about her . . . She's talking shit.'

Sultan was mortified and yet neither the girl nor Mr Racaille moved an inch, eyes locked onto each other.

'Impersonal? Tell me . . . tell me how it's impersonal. I'm curious.' Mr Racaille, now smiling, was intrigued.

'I don't know . . . I mean, it just seems . . . you know, impersonal. I mean if you're gonna get rid of someone, you'd want it to be . . . close. Intimate.'

Mr Racaille stared deep into her eyes and held her stare. She stared right back at him, dead still. *Don't flinch or he'll know you're shitting yourself. Don't move or he'll whip that impersonal tool-of-death out and spray bullets into you,* she instructed herself.

The longest silence was broken by a shrill chuckle. 'Hahahah! I like you! You're all right. Hahaha! What a girl! Hey, Sultan, you watch out for her—your lady's something. You're all right, mademoiselle, you're all right. Hey, have this one on me—compliments to you, mademoiselle.'

With that he stuffed a bag into her hand and walked away laughing. Sultan stood there dumbfounded.

That was the last time he took her with him to pick up.

STUPIDITY

Because I loved you,
I told myself,
that having the worst parts
of you was better
than having nothing at all.
Because I loved you,
I told myself,
that having your rough edges
cut me open
each time I got too close
was better than not having you at all.
Because I loved you,
I told myself,
it was better to deep-throat
your half-truths and
gag on them
than not having you at all.
Because I loved you, I told myself.

TWENTY-SEVEN

DICK GRAB AT MONTE CRISTO

It wasn't her first time there, maybe her fifth or sixth. She loved that place—Café Monte Cristo on the Champs-Élysées. After dinner service, salsa and merengue music blasted through speakers that lined the narrow dance floor as carefree patrons laughed and swayed their hips, sipping sugary cocktails. At sixteen, it was a magical place—a place that never ID'd her, a place where she could dance the Saturday night away with her best gal-pal Sophia without a care in the world.

'I'd like to see how far that tattoo goes down.'

Hot alcohol breath on her skin. A man's voice coming from behind her. The girl turned around and saw a thirty-something man licking his lips.

'Excuse me? What?'

'Your tattoo, on your back—I want to see how far it goes down. Maybe you'll show me?'

He edged closer, groin thrusting forward as if his dick was leading the way. He wasn't even looking at her face; all the words were directed at her ass.

The girl raised an eyebrow and threw him her unimpressed resting bitch face, shrugged off his comment and walked towards the bar. She figured that should be enough for Mr Cock to get the message that she wasn't interested and to leave her alone.

But it wasn't enough. Even before the girl could reach the bar, greedy hands grabbed her ass, then her hips, then slid down to her crotch.

'I want to feel my cock against you when you dance.'

Same sour alcohol breath against her ear. Something in her switched. Those words, those hands, that fucking breath—they flicked a switch. Whether it was the copious amount of tequila she had drunk or whether it was that she simply had had enough of being groped and spoken to like a piece of meat, she flipped. She swung around, squeezed his balls as hard as she could and hissed words that spat out naturally.

'Keep your small dick and hands the fuck away from me or I'll fucking rip your fucking balls off!' she hissed. Albeit they all came out in English instead of French, she was sure this time he got the message.

Mr Cock went pale. His shoulders hunched over; his hands clamped together as if in prayer for her to release him of his agony. A small crowd had gathered around them, some in shock whilst others sniggered and whispered. She let go and started to walk away, trembling from the adrenalin. No less than a metre away from her, Mr Cock began to projectile vomit a whole array of abuse at her.

'Whore. Slut. Bitch. Dick tease. Psycho bitch. Cunt. Fucking crazy whore.'

Funny how they grow a pair when you can't grab them. Sophia sprinted up to her, stunned at the girl's rash gutsiness.

'That was amazing!'

'You saw that?'

'Yeah, I was right there! I can't believe you did that, you okay? You're shaking!'

'I . . . I'm okay. I don't know what came over me. I'm . . . I'm quite scared.'

'What? Why? He's left! That guy was shitting himself!'

'I guess . . . I don't know. I guess . . . well, what if he's waiting outside for me when I leave? What if he hits me on the head, drags me somewhere and rapes me?'

'What? No. There's nothing to worry about, that's not going to happen. He's gone.'

'I hope so.'

'Besides, you were a total badass just then. He wouldn't dare.'

'I hope so . . . I really hope so, Sophia.'

She never went back to Monte Cristo after that.

TWENTY-EIGHT

DON'T SWING YOUR LEGS IN BOIS DE BOULOGNE

It was dark. Yellow shards of streetlamp light pierced through the trees, disguising everything ugly, seedy and urine-saturated about Paris. They were waiting for Sultan. She didn't particularly want to be in the middle of Bois de Boulogne this late at night. She didn't really want to get in the fancy SUV that Mo had driven to pick her up and take her to the middle of nowhere with no means of getting home. She didn't really want to be waiting with her boyfriend's best friend, whose sleazy smile and gluttonous hands made her insides recoil. She heard about Bois de Boulogne— a place for prostitutes, junkies, the homeless and everyone else in between. A place for the trash and rejects of society, and now her. *I am trash. I am total garbage. I guess I belong here too.*

It was chillier than previous nights. The late August breeze sliced through the thick summer heat, cutting its way through all that was suffocating. It caught her hair. Her massive frizz of black roots and cheap bronze. A DIY job gone terribly wrong. To her, it was hooker-chic. She somehow took pride in how cheap and trashy she looked. It went with the package. *I am trash. I am total garbage. Even my hair is trash.*

They hid in the shadows, obscured by the trees as Mo rolled a joint. Scratching. Rubbing. Grinding. Rolling. Licking. No words spoken. A flicker of a lighter. Inhale, exhale. Mo's hand grabbed her by the arm as they zigzagged through more trees before arriving at a ping-pong table. Big leather jacket arms wrapped around her and planted her on top of the table. The cold from the table penetrated deep through her trousers and seeped into her crotch. She felt the cold sinking into her spine. She'll remember that kind of cold for ever after tonight.

She couldn't see much except for the orange glow of the joint and the silhouette of Mo's physique. She could see the outline of her legs as they started to swing. She was stoned again. *Don't fall over. Don't fall off this table.* She clenched onto the edge as her fingertips went pale from holding on too tightly. He stepped into her, right between her swinging legs. His mouth opened and breathed smoke into hers. Large ravenous arms gripped onto her thighs, hard enough to bruise, as he pulled her closer and closer to him. Rapacious hands tugged down at her top, pulling at her trousers. His hands were everywhere. Thick slobbery lips thrusted against hers.

'Stop it. Stop! Come on. Stop it!'

But he didn't stop. Of course, he didn't. Why would he? Girls who say 'stop' and 'no' really mean 'go' and 'yes'. Had she forgotten how to shout?

'Stop it! I said fucking stop it! Back the fuck off, Mo!'

She pushed him but her arms were too heavy. Floppy arms. Stoned arms. *How the hell did I get here?* Palms smacked and grabbed her ass. Knees barged between her legs as he spread her and shoved himself up against her. She was shaking, not from the cold of the ping-pong table but from utter terror. *This is it. This is the nightmare you have dreaded all your life. What are you going to do now, girl?* Internal monologues aren't going to help now.

'Fuck. Who the fuck is calling now?' Mo shouted.

Nokia 3210 flashed luminous in the darkness. It was Sultan calling to see where they were. He was just around the corner.

'Fuck,' said Mo, smiled at her sordidly through his yellow teeth, 'Well, I guess we'll have to finish this off another time, won't we? When we won't be interrupted.'

He let out a forced laugh and stared at her threateningly.

'We're cool, right? 'Cause you know, if you tell, you're fucked because I'll be fucked. Don't forget, Sweet Cheeks, I know where you live, and I know how to have you,' he threatened her through a sleazy smile.

She looked right back at him, doing her best to put on a brave, defiant face, holding back the tears and screams.

'Yeah. We're cool,' she replied.

But they definitely were not—she was panicked.

She always felt that as a woman she lived in two terrors simultaneously. The first was to go unnoticed, not seen nor looked at. The second was to be noticed, seen and even gawked at. She didn't know there was a third—to be unheard no matter how loudly she screamed.

TWENTY-NINE

FORGOTTEN TAMPON DENT

It hurt more than usual, the sex. Something was wrong. Something was bruised, something swollen—something deep inside. But he didn't tell her. He said nothing as he stabbed her with his cock, jamming her forgotten tampon deeper and deeper into her.

Post-coital trip to the toilet followed by a dull ache that quickly seeped into a throbbing pain. She tried to subdue the pangs by pushing the heels of her palms against her uterus and pubic bone. Panic. Heart pounding. Then the realisation of her stupidity and carelessness—sex with a forgotten tampon. Short-stubbly-fingers-search-party for the all-important string. *It can't be that bad. It must happen to other women too. It must. Probably happens all the time.* Thoughts turned into lies of comfort that she told herself. *Gotcha!* She found the string but was too scared to pull at it.

It felt stuck. Stuck and clogged and dry. She knew she had to yank it out at some point, that she couldn't stay on the toilet for the rest of her life. She tugged at the string. A jammed excruciating pain followed by more panic and more lies to herself. She had wanted to call out to Sultan for help. *What's he going to do? He's probably already passed out or asleep. Stupid girl. Fucking idiot. You've really gotten yourself into a jam now! He must have felt something. He couldn't have not felt anything. Why didn't he say something? Why did he just keep going? Why didn't I say anything? Too late now. You're stuck with a tampon string between your legs and too afraid to pull.*

Because she was too afraid to pull, she decided to try and push it out like a giant constipated shit, but it didn't budge. *I can't live in this toilet.* She took a deep breath. *Three-two-one-pull!* With a hard yank, the tampon came out. Still in her hand, she caught sight of it. There weren't the same colours of crimson red and deep maroons on stained cotton. Instead, stuck onto the top of the tampon was a thick layer of pink human tissue about the size of a pinkie-nail on the side. She studied it, smelt it and touched it. It was soft and of substance. *What is that?* Her stoic trance was broken as soon as she flushed her tampon down the toilet. The wretched pain inside her was paralysing.

When she got home, she stuck two investigative fingers up herself. *There. Right there. What is that?* Where her cervix sat, there was a dent. It was sore and swollen to touch. She could feel it—something that was once there, isn't there any more. It was on the tampon now making its way down the Parisian sewage system somewhere. She was left with a dent, an absence, no bigger than a pinkie nail. Sultan had left a dent on the barriers into her womanhood, a dent in her that would never grow back.

She would go on to tell herself that she was lucky that nothing got infected, that she was lucky enough not to have to tell her mother and to have to explain how it had happened. These were just some of the lies she told herself as a teenager.

THIRTY

ABANDONED IDIOTS

She had stopped caring, stopped caring that she was smoking too much cannabis or that whole days would be lost in Luca's room. Stopped caring what their friends assumed was going on between them because theirs was a relationship that was beyond the physical. She was safe with Luca. Safe that no one and nothing could hurt her there because it would just be her, Luca, their big bag of marijuana and her Zippo. Nothing and no one else.

Whole afternoons of whole weekends and school holidays melted away through the same ritual. The same text message invitation. Bring your Zippo. The same Cheshire cat smile that always welcomed her as he opened the door and the same greeting:

'Hey, Foxy.'

Met with the same reply.

'Hey, Luca'.

The same quiet steps to the lift up three floors to his 'room'. ('Floor'.) No words were ever exchanged as she sank onto his day bed, dropped her bag on the floor and watched Luca start rolling joints to the rhythm of lounge music in the background. The all-too-familiar sound of her Zippo flicking open. Inhale, hold, exhale, repeat.

This ritual repeated itself throughout the entire school year. At first, their conversations were superficial debates about random topics. Later they learnt to share spasms of hysterical laughter as they watched every single stoner film available on VHS. But more often than not, their time together was spent in companionable silence. Luca was the first person she had ever been able to share silence with and feel completely secure.

On one particular evening whilst she was sprawled out next to Luca on his bed fully clothed, he suddenly stopped blowing smoke rings into the ceiling and propped himself up.

'Can I ask you something?' he said.

'Yeah. Go on.'

Feeling like she had no endoskeleton, she struggled to even turn her head towards him.

'Do you ever miss him?' he asked.

'Who?'

'Your dad.'

Pause. Big sigh. The girl hadn't paid much thought to her estranged father ever since her paternal grandmother doubted her legitimate existence.

'No . . . Erm . . . No. I guess not . . . I mean, can you miss something that was never really there? I mean, I feel that something's missing but, I don't know. I don't remember him enough to miss him. You know? What about you? Do you miss him? Your dad, I mean?'

'I don't think so. I'm not sure. I remember him, I remember a lot of things. Growing up . . . well, it was hard. No amount of money could make that shit better. Money still can't, you know?' he said.

'Yeah . . . I think so. I guess it's like you're trying to fill up this hole, this emptiness with booze, fucking, food, weed. It just won't go away . . . I guess that's how I feel most of the time,' she sighed.

'Exactly.'

Long pause.

'Hey, do you think you've got family you don't know about?' he asked her.

'Sure, I imagine my dad setting up a sperm franchise around the world. You?'

The girl's thoughts went to her father, to the half-sisters she had never met from his previous marriage, to the possibility she might even have more siblings out there, a whole army of abandoned boys and girls.

'Yeah, those poor abandoned idiots. Ha! That's us too, you know—abandoned idiots.' Luca tried to laugh it off.

As she sat up, he placed his hand on hers and brushed her hair back. He saw her and she saw him and in that moment of shared vulnerability, his hot cotton-mouth lips pressed against hers. A deep embrace, it felt oddly comforting. When the kissing stopped, Luca smiled. Not a Cheshire cat smile, but something different, something honest. It was the first and only time she saw his truest, sincerest smile.

'Hey, does your girlfriend know about this? I mean, do you ever talk to Emily about it?'

'Nah. I can't talk to her about shit like this, she won't get it.'

They continued to lie there for hours. Two abandoned idiots in a hazy embrace, staring at the ceiling, exhaling smoke.

THIRTY-ONE

PAVILION SEX SHOW

She wasn't used to the late September Cumbrian chill. It was a lot cooler than what she was used to, and she had never been a fan of the cold. This cold was different, a humid kind of cold—one that sank into her clothes and deep into her bones. *If this is September, I don't even want to imagine what February will be like.* She thought to herself as she waited outside the Boarding House entrance for her new friends who had invited her to the Pavilion. The Pavilion was exactly that—an outdoor pavilion at the end of a rugby pitch in the next village, where her new friends were taking her drinking. A very different world from the salsa bars, upscale clubs, brasseries or even Luca's home in Paris. In fact, everything about Cumbria felt at odds with what she had been used to. The seemingly endless emerald fields, persistent lingering smell of manure and total absence of any sign of urban life overwhelmed the girl so much that upon her first day in Kendal, she burst into tears. *I can't believe I had volunteered to come here. What was I thinking? I can't believe I'm stuck here! What did I sign myself up for?* Her mother laughed at how childish the girl was being.

The girl certainly felt childish now as she mulled over the idea of having to sneak around and drink alcohol outdoors. *But it's so cold!* It did not fill her with much elation but with nothing else to do on a Friday evening, she decided to go along.

As she waited for her new friends outside, Jones strutted up towards her.

'Hey, got a spare fag?' Jones asked. Jones was in Year Ten. They had met on their first day and shared a game of pool. The girl had initially thought that Jones was rather attractive, but that was before the boy had opened his mouth. His words and mannerisms betrayed him as he tried dreadfully to appear older than he was. But he was just another teenage boy—emphasis on <u>boy</u>. The teenage boys in Cumbria seemed like kids compared with those in Paris who seemed like adults without even trying.

The girl raised an eyebrow. 'Yeah. Sure.'

She handed over her pack of cigarettes and offered him one. 'What's with the red backwards cap, Fred Durst?' she laughed.

'That was actually the look I was going for,' Jones replied proudly adjusting his cap.

'Oh.'

'Not a Limp Bizkit fan then?' Jones gave off a sly, cheeky smile as if to be flirtatious.

'I'd rather stick blunt spoons in my ears.'

The girl rolled her eyes and searched for her new friends to arrive so she didn't have to play civil with Jones.

'Oh. Okay, erm, so, where you off to tonight then?'

'Eh, a bunch of us are going to the Pavilion.' *Please don't invite yourself. Please don't come.*

'Cool! Can I come?' Jones was quick to ask for an invitation which she wasn't prepared to dish out.

'Eh, not sure. It's just a small group of us.'

'Hey, Jones, you coming with us then?' said a voice. Sam's invitation popped out of the blue as he walked towards them. *Damn it!*

'For sure.'

Jones licked his lips and winked at the girl. *Yuck. Double yuck.*

There were six of them: Sam, Kayley, Charlie, Ed, her . . . and Jones. They walked the 1.5 miles to the closest village and stopped at the only Spar within a 5-mile radius.

'You're going to need to get the booze for us.' Sam stopped her outside the shop.

'What? Why?'

'You look the oldest out of us lot.'

'You mean they ID you here?'

The girl was surprised, as she had never been ID'd for alcohol before. It wasn't a custom on the Continent nor in Hong Kong. It had never even occurred to her to carry one with her.

'Yeah, they do! And they know me in there, so they know I'm not fucking eighteen yet.'

'But I'm not eighteen yet. I don't have ID.'

'Yeah, but you look older. And to be fair, when I first saw you, I thought you were a new teacher, so you're getting the booze.'

'Oh. Thanks.'

She wasn't quite sure how to take that, whether she should be flattered for looking more grown-up—after all, that's what most teenage girls aimed for—or whether she should be offended for looking old.

'Okay, so, don't forget vodka for me. Get the cheapest one, I'm skint.'

'And my Smirnoff Ice!' requested Charlie.

Charlie was only thirteen and the girl wasn't sure how she felt about being an accomplice to a thirteen-year-old's getting smashed. But she thought back to when she was only thirteen and those Friday nights with Lara smoking cannabis. *Meh. Whatever.*

The group started to shove money into the girl's hand which was also a very unfamiliar experience. Back in Paris, friends would cover a tab at their table in an upscale club or if they were at a house party, everyone would just bring something to share—a bottle of whisky, champagne, a good vintage Bordeaux, even gin. No one ever handed cash over to their friends and if they did, it was never done in front of her—the boys simply took care of it.

'Guys, erm . . . this is a lot of booze you want me to get. I'm not so sure . . .'

'That's fair.' Sam nodded his head. 'How about a deal? You get us booze and I give you my weed. You can have the whole bag.'

Sam took it out of his pocket to show her as proof. He clearly knew how to strike a good bargain, so the girl agreed. Since arriving in the UK, she hadn't made any weed connections, so she appreciated Sam's offer all the more.

'I'm coming with you. I've got ID just in case,' said Kayley, who had a fake NUS student ID card but was reluctant to use it as it was an obvious counterfeit.

'And what about me?' queried Jones.

'You got cash? No? So, you'll get what's given to you,' snapped Kayley as she stormed into the shop. The girl liked Kayley.

As the sun began to slip into the darkness, the group settled in at the Pavilion with their poisons of choice. The girl had never gone out with a group of English friends before and was astonished to see how quickly they tossed back their booze, giving full meaning to the term 'binge drinking'. Sam, true to his word, handed over his weed to the girl and before long the group had coupled off.

It was like nothing she had ever seen before. On the one side of the Pavilion was Sam, totally off his face and stripped practically naked as Charlie straddled him with nothing but her bra on, all in plain sight and in the damp cold. On the other side were Kayley and Ed, who were a little more civilised as their bodies rocked backwards and forwards underneath their coats and jackets. Then there was the girl—tequila in one hand, joint in the other. She tried not to pay too much attention to the live sex-show as she wasn't sure what the social protocol was for gawking at her new peers. *Do I watch? Do I look away? But I can't, they are right in front of me. Do I go back? This is very strange.*

She would have been content had it not been for Jones' persistent lack of personal-space awareness as he scooted uncomfortably close to her. Each time she shuffled down the bench, he edged closer. Had she been single she would perhaps have toyed with the notion, but she missed Sultan and she had committed herself to him. Sultan with his masculine broad shoulders, that chiselled jawline and that manly Dior Fahrenheit cologne smell. She felt a warmth between her legs every time she thought of him, but the smell of Jones' Lynx deodorant and Fructose hair gel invaded her private thoughts, the smell of a boy.

'Did I tell you you're looking especially fine tonight?' Jones shuffled closer to her, again.

'Firstly, the term "fine" as far as I understand is not a term often used here in the UK. It's an American term. You're not American, so why try to sound like one? And secondly, Jones, it's not going to happen. I have a boyfriend and have no intention of cheating. Thirdly, stop edging closer, you're killing my buzz.'

'Oh.'

He was startled, as he wasn't used to being rejected and certainly not in that manner but decided to shrug off her comment.

'Umm, can I have some of that?' Jones asked, trying to regain some face.

'Yeah, sure.'

She handed over her joint. Jones did what all non-smokers who pretended to smoke do—suck the smoke in, keep it in the mouth and blow it out in a ball of mess. She had seen it done so many times back in Paris with all the tweeny groupies who surrounded Luca pretending to dabble in cannabis. Luca would just laugh it off. He found it hilarious and enjoyed the attention. She missed Luca. She missed his warm room, she missed melting hours away with him, nestled on his day bed. She missed their long silences.

'You don't smoke, do you?'

'What? Sure, I do. Look—'

He did it again but this time it really annoyed her; he was wasting her weed and she didn't like wasters.

'Stop that. You're wasting my joint and I don't share with non-smokers. Give it back.'

She snatched it off him, inhaled and sat back, watching the sex show in front of her.

Luca, u won't believe what I'm seein rite now. Live sex show. New friends fuckin in front of me.

She texted on her Nokia 3210. *Boarding school is going to be very different. Very different.*

Growing up is losing some illusions, in order to acquire others.

Virginia Woolf

THIRTY-TWO

TATTOO BETS

'So, this is what you want. Are you sure?'

'Yes.'

'This is what you want tattooed?'

'Yes. And I'd like it here, just above the pelvis.'

'Er . . . ok. Sit.'

She had never chickened out of a bet before and she wasn't going to start now. Stupidly stubborn, she had to win. Every. Single. Time. She had to win no matter the cost, even if it meant getting the name of her boyfriend Sultan tattooed on her pelvis. That was what he wanted. That was what he needed for her to prove her love to him and that she had truly forgiven him for cheating on her with Nadia whilst high on E.

February half-term, back in Paris for the week. After extensive love letters, phone calls, text messages, love songs and everything else in between, Sultan had managed to slither his way back into her life. But it wasn't enough. He wanted her to prove her love. He wanted her to be entirely his, only his, for ever. He needed her to prove her love. What started out as a joke after too many joints, turned into a bet.

'Get my name tattooed on you,' he said out of nowhere.

They were sitting in his rococo living room with the flat to themselves as usual.

'What? You crazy? What? Tattoo your name? Fuck off!'

'I'm serious. I bet you don't love me enough to get it done.'

'That's not fair.'

'Then bet with me. If you really love me, you'll do it.'

It was the stupidest, most foolish bet she had ever accepted in her entire life (to date). *What a fucking idiot.*

Now she was branded, permanently. Every time she got into the shower, every time she got dressed, every time she went to the toilet, she would see his name: Sultan. Carved with ink, etched into her skin, for ever. *Stupid fucking stubborn idiot. You just had to do it, didn't you?* She scolded herself as she contemplated taking a lit cigarette to her flesh and burning the whole thing off. *No. It'll serve as a reminder. Tattooing a name is the worst fucking idea ever. Couldn't have learnt from Johnny Depp, could you?*

By the time her next visit to Paris had come around, Sultan and the girl had broken up and her radical gesture of loving devotion was now rendered utterly pointless. Sultan's inability to keep his dick in his pants and the girl's total lack of trust in the man-child she used to love had eroded their once-loving relationship. After a couple of months of mind-games, blame-games, shouting matches and silent treatments, she reminded herself of what she had written to him: 'The longer I stay with you, the less I love myself'. She ended their turbulent relationship. By Easter break, Sultan was already onto his latest squeeze, Emily.

Emily. Emily with her perfect blonde hair and the lustrous green eyes. Emily with the perfect face, tiny waist, voluptuous breasts. Emily with the manicured nails, stainless white teeth and that Hollywood smile. Emily with the wealthy parents who afforded her a confidence the girl only dreamed of one day growing. Emily who had once giggled and flicked her blonde hair flirtatiously at Sultan, as the girl stood by like the irrelevant bystander that she was. Emily who had become Sultan's girlfriend suspiciously quickly after the girl had finally broken things off. Emily. Emily, whose name the girl was told, was now tattooed on Sultan's forearm in Arabic. The girl had to see it for herself. When Luca mentioned it in passing, the girl could not believe it. But there it was, right there across his olive-skinned forearm.

'Nice tattoo. What does it say?'

The girl eyeballed his left arm as she stubbed out her cigarette, clenching her jaw.

'Ummah. It means "mother" in Arabic.'

Quick response from Sultan. He had obviously rehearsed this in his mind several times.

'Oh, I see. You sure it's not Emily in Arabic?' she said, raising an eyebrow.

'So, how long are you back in town for?' Sultan quickly changed the subject. He couldn't admit he had gotten Emily's name tattooed on him. *Coward. Chicken shit.*

The girl immediately thought of her tattoo of his name on her pelvis. *This is some sick tattoo love triangle. This is fucking ridiculous.* As she beat herself up in her mind, the girl imagined herself marching into his kitchen, grabbing an iron and burning him off her.

'Why did you call me to come over, Sultan?' she sighed.

'I wanted to see you. Luca told me you were in town. I missed you, can't we be friends?'

'Huh.' She paused. 'And what would Emily say?'

'Nothing. She won't say anything. You and I . . . we have a history, Habibti.'

'Don't call me that. Not any more, not again. That's for Emily, not me.'

Yes, Emily. Emily whose framed headshot stared back at her as she fucked her boyfriend on the same bed they had all shared—all three of them. She didn't know why she did it; why she kissed him back, why she wrapped her legs around him as he lifted her off the chair, why she let him undress her, why she straddled him, why to any of it. People do extraordinarily stupid things when they have been hurt, stupider still when they've been scorned by someone they used to love.

Straddling Sultan, she didn't take her eyes off Emily's portrait. *If I stare at you whilst fucking him, would I also be fucking you?*

When they were done, Sultan, she would later learn, dropped the girl off in his father's white Mercedes-Benz then drove straight to Emily's home, picked her up, took her back to his place and fucked her in his unmade bed.

Six months later, in the middle of the Boarding House car park, the girl would have to confront the fact she was a willing accomplice to the emotional meltdown of an innocent girl. Luca had called her up, saying it was urgent that they talked.

'What are you saying, Luca?'

'You should speak to her.'

'Who?'

'Emily.'

'Why? She's not gonna want to talk to me.'

'She does. I think you both need to speak to each other. You've both been fucked over by Sultan. Come on, just talk to her. Emily's here with me.'

'No—don't put her on the ph—'

'Hello?'

'Hi, Emily,' gulped the girl.

'Yeah . . . Hi.'

Emily was already sobbing, her voice barely recognisable. This could not have been more awkward—being on the phone, with her ex-boyfriend's now ex-girlfriend, who is now dating your smoking buddy.

'I'm sorry, Emily. What I did to you . . . with him. I'm . . . I'm sorry.'

The girl was and is terrible at apologies. The words tasted bitter and sour coming out of her mouth, but she knew it was the right thing to do. *Fucking conscience, fuck you.*

'I'm . . . I . . . I am so . . . sor . . . sorry too.' Loud sobbing.

The girl had to pull the phone away from her ear as she waited for Emily to calm down.

'You've got nothing to be sorry about, Emily.'

'Yes. Yes, I do. When you two were still together . . . and . . . and you were away at school, like in England. Before you came back for Easter break. We . . . ummm . . . Sultan and I, we were fucking.' Big sob. 'We were fucking behind your back and I knew. I knew you two were still together and I did it anyway.'

Long pause.

Suddenly, flashes of images she had desperately rammed down the prison of her memory palace had escaped. Images running rampant in her mind. Horrific unspeakable images of what Sultan had done to her during that same Easter break. Everything inside her burned. Everything inside her collapsed, hurt.

'You still there? Hello?' Emily still sobbing.

'Yeah . . . just put Luca back on the phone. Now.'

'Yeah, I'm here,' responded Luca.

'Don't tell her. Don't tell her what happened on Easter break. Don't tell anyone. Promise me, Luca, you can't—'

'I know. I know.'

Click.

THIRTY-THREE

SOMEBODY THAT SHE USED TO LOVE

Heavy eyes.
Heavier limbs.
On your stomach
the same bed
you made love in.
Now another girl's perfume
saturates the sheets.
It's time to get out of here.
Don't lay there
on your stomach
with somebody you used to love.
Remember just what kind of
person you're lying
next to.
The person you used to love.
His brazen smile as you ask
words in slow motion
pulled out of ash-dry mouth.
'What did you give me to smoke?'
Don't just lay there

on your stomach

with somebody that you used to love.

NO.

STOP.

Words he couldn't hear.

Words he chose not to hear,

as he lowered himself

into you

and all you could do

was lay paralytic

spread-eagled on your stomach.

Cunt burning.

Tears streaming.

Muffled no's and stops

under the person you used to love.

You tell yourself it'll be over soon

so think of something better

than needing to get out of here.

Because it's too late

when you're on your stomach

under the person you used to love

who doesn't understand no.

By the time it was over, Sultan peeled his sweaty, salty body off her and passed out. How much time had passed between The Incident and her ability to muster enough strength to stand up and crawl out of his apartment? She didn't know. It was the small hours of Saturday morning and the room was still drenched in darkness. Sunrise was a long way away and her home seemed even further. Somehow, she had managed to call a taxi, get in, get home and get into bed. The entire journey fuelled by a single thought—*get home*.

When she awoke, it was dark and silent. Everything hurt, pried open, aching, smashed in. How much time had elapsed since getting home and waking up? She didn't know. As she sat up, she listened for signs of her mother upstairs. But the flat was silent. *Good. No one's home. She's probably still at work.* There was no way her mother could ever know. No way her mother could ever find out. No way.

Maybe a hot bath would help. Something was chafed, it burned. Something has been damaged down there. Something terribly, hideously wrong had happened. The hot water scalded her raw skin. Fragments of The Incident stabbed through her mind. *I can't think about that right now. I need to wake up and clean up.* She felt poisoned. She had been smoking copious amounts of cannabis for years and never had she had such a reaction—lethargic to the point of being paralytic. *You know what happened to you. You know it. Say it. Say what happened to you.* More fragments from The Incident. She closed her eyes and fell back into the bathtub. Screeching screams of horror. *What is that fucking screaming?* It was her, head underwater, screaming. *What did you do? What did you do to me? What did you do, Sultan?*

A few days had passed and the girl went to find refuge in Luca, who could tell immediately something about the girl was hideously wrong.

'That wasn't just weed he gave you.' Luca shook his head. His face frozen in shock at what Sultan did to the girl. 'It would have been laced with something.'

'Something? Like what?'

'Don't know. Could be anything. Heroin, cocaine . . . crack. Anything.' Big sigh. 'Have you told anyone about what happened?'

Luca wanted to look at the girl but kept his gaze lowered, as if ashamed on Sultan's behalf.

'No. No one, just you.'

'I just don't get why he would do that. Why? Especially to you. I just don't . . . I don't know. Fuck.'

Just as Luca was about to light his joint, he paused and put it down.

'You need to tell someone.'

The girl just nodded lifelessly as she crawled into the foetal position, nestling herself next to Luca on his daybed. Wasn't she telling someone now?

'Can I stay here awhile? Can you stay here with me?'

'Sure,' he said as he brushed her hair off her forehead. 'Stay as long as you want.'

Luca didn't smoke the whole time whilst the girl stayed with him.

The girl would never know exactly what was given to her to smoke that night nor why Sultan did it. She would never know why he drugged her and ignored her muffled cries to stop. But a lot of things would also go unanswered for some time, and when she finally mustered up enough courage to open her internal door to survey the carnage, she decided to write it all down.

I shouldn't have gone to his home. I should have left when the others left. I shouldn't have smoked with him. Was it my fault? It was my fault. What did he give me? I should have tasted a difference, shouldn't I?

Yes, I wore a strappy top and low-cut jeans. Yes, I wore a black lace thong. Did that matter? It mattered. Right?

He was my boyfriend. He loved me! He wrote epic songs and poems dedicated to me. Did that matter? It mattered. Right?

What did he give me? Why? Did he even know?

I was too stoned. It was my fault. I should have left when the rest of them did.

Did he plan it? Why? Did he even know? Is it still r**e if it's your ex-boyfriend? No, that can't happen right? He was MY boyfriend.

We LOVED each other so intensely once. No, it wasn't that R word. It was my fault. I shouldn't have gone over. I shouldn't have smoked. I shouldn't have worn a strappy top and low-cut jeans.

No, it couldn't have been that R word. Ex-boyfriends can't r**e you, right?

When I inserted my tampon in yesterday it felt funny. It hurt. It hurt badly—right at the top so I stuck my fingers in.

That dent that he caused. He caused that—feels ages ago now.

Is it normal that it's uneven when it used to be? He did that.

What did he do?

WHAT DID YOU DO, SULTAN?

How could this happen in a city as beautiful as Paris?

LIKE YOU

My mother never warned
Me about
Man-children like
You.
Whose touch made
Girls like me
Spread her legs
As she stuffed
Her mouth full
Of you.

She never warned
Me about
Man-children like you
Who'd break girls
Like me
Down.
And inject them
With half-truths
That turned them
Into junkies
High on fabricated
Love.

She never warned
Me about
Man-children like you
Who took away
Pieces of me
Until there was nothing
Left.
Not even my
Own voice
To say no.
To say STOP.

THIRTY-FOUR

MAUSOLEUM OF LOVERS

Her body once so pure, so beautiful, now became a mausoleum of lovers and with each one, she became a little emptier, a little number, a little colder. *In a world that divided women into Eves and Marys, I'd rather be a Lilith. Fuck it. Fuck 'em all.*

She was giving herself to anyone and everyone who wanted her. It seemed to her to be the English way. She'd take one by the hand, lead them behind the Sixth Form Common Room, push them onto a bench, hike up her skirt and take what she wanted. She figured if she took what she wanted, if she treated each one of them as her willing human-sized dildo, she could fuck out the trauma of what happened to her. She would be in charge. She would be the one holding the consent between her legs as she sat on her nameless lovers.

It didn't matter to her that it was freezing cold and that they were outdoors, nor that they could be caught by the Boarding House staff. It didn't matter to her that rumours had circulated around the Sixth Form that she was an easy lay. How could she have been an easy lay if she never so much as lay down? She never lay on her stomach, she never lay on her back either; not after what happened. No. She wasn't going to relinquish control. Control—that is what she told herself as she gave herself up to the night, to the moon, to the stars, with a silent prayer that with each fuck she could somehow forget what Sultan did to her. *What within me must die for me to go on living? Tell me.*

THIRTY-FIVE

NO DEPRESSION

'What is wrong with you?'

'I don't know, Mum.' The girl shrugged stoically.

'Must be something wrong. Something wrong with <u>you</u>. All this writing on your desk. Death. Dying. Anger. Sorrow. What is all this, huh? So dark, so miserable. Something wrong with you. Not normal, not correct.'

'I don't know. Maybe I'm depressed . . . I don't know.'

'Depressed? What depressed? Not depressed, no depression. Depression Western disease. No such thing.'

'Okay, if you say so.'

'Depression Western disease. Too much time on your hands, your life too comfortable for you, too easy. If you poor and starving, nothing to eat, then no time for depression. No depression.'

'Okay, Ma, if you say so.'

THIRTY-SIX

TEARS IN LANCASTER

'Tears in Heaven'. She fucking hated that song. No disrespect to Eric Clapton. On the one hand, it's one of the most beautifully melancholic songs that relates a deep longing and a solemn remorse. On the other, it's a song that would always remind her of what a pathetic combination the taste of bile and hospital bleach is when you're seventeen and on a hospital bed after what they would later label a suicide attempt.

A pinching feeling had awoken her. A pinching on the raw cuticles of an over-bitten left index finger. Eyes travelled to the source of the irritation: a pale grey plastic clip linked to a heart rate monitor. Eyes travelled further to her hand and to her exposed wrist. *Busted. Stripped.* Her trophies of pain were out in the open for all the world to see in the cold hard hospital light. All her bruises, slashes and scabs: her cherished sordid secret, long hidden under oversized long-sleeved shirts and leather wristbands, now lay exposed. *There's no going back now. They all know. You're exposed. You've been busted. They're onto you, and now they're going to try to fix you. They will try to cure you. You're fucked now, girl. Fucked.*

They would go on to label this as a suicide attempt. They would go on to tell her that she had severe depression and required immediate professional help. They would press medication upon her—medication that would help her, medication that would balance her out, medication that would make things easier. She didn't want easier; she wanted silence. *Is this all really necessary? I just wanted it to be quiet, just for a while.*

They did not believe her that suicide was not her intention. All the girl wanted was for the entire world to be silenced, just for a second. A single moment of pure blissful silence, of utter detachment from any thoughts or feelings, of anything at all. She was exhausted. Exhausted by having to portray herself as an incredibly confident and outspoken girl 'with lots of potential' whilst doing battle with the monsters that inhabited her mind.

This exhaustion had drilled a hole through her that no amount of alcohol, weed or fucking could fill. Even the skin cutting and the wrist banging that had once temporarily distracted her from her mental pain stopped having any effect. The hole got deeper and bigger as it grew into a monster abyss. And as Nietzsche had put it, the moment she stared down this abyss, the abyss stared right back at her. It was terrifying. She realised she had nothing to root her, to peg her to the ground and sooner or later she would just be swept away into nothingness—the opposite of being. All the while, the monsters in her head were banging on her psyche—it had become unbearably noisy up there.

I am toxic waste. With a cocktail of nurofen, ibuprofen, paracetamol and aspirin which she chased down with as much vodka as she could stomach, she snail-trailed her way back to the Boarding House. *This is it. This is when the abyss stares back at you, girl. It's coming . . . the silence. Yes, the silence. This is it.* But it didn't work. The silence did not come. *You can't even do this right. This is really quite pathetic. You are pathetic.* Nothing had gone to plan, not even when she sat down in the middle of the road where she had the misfortune to run into Mr Mandrell, Head of Boarding.

'What on earth do you think you're doing sat on the road?' Mr Mandrell stomped out of his car, shouting at her out of serious concern.

'I'm waiting for a car to come and run me over.'

'You're an idiot! Get in the bloody car. Get in! Now!' he roared at her.

'No. I'm not going. You can't make me. I'm not fucking going!'

'Stupid, silly, silly girl!' Mr Mandrell shook his head in dismay, got back in his car and drove off.

No convincing this girl. She crawled the 1.5 miles back to the school grounds, stumbled into the office and collapsed on the chair in front of Mr Mandrell's desk. Everything began to spin in a haze. Mr Mandrell had been waiting for her all this time. Phone receiver in hand, his fat stumpy fingers hammered the buttons. *I guess I'm being taken to the hospital. It's definitely not going to be quiet there either. Fucking retard. You fucked up now.*

Had she fallen asleep? Or had she just zoned out? Pinching irritation on her left index finger. She was suddenly very aware of how thin the mattress was, how the thin blanket that covered her smelt like stale bleach and how her dry lips felt sealed shut. Bitter bile in her mouth lined with fuzzy teeth—the remnants of vomit. Her eyes crusty from tears she couldn't remember shedding but somehow, she felt at peace. Somehow, she felt serene. *Silence. Finally, thank you.* But she spoke too quickly. Her Nokia 3310 Prodigy Breathe ringtone pierced the air, pierced her silence. Did she jump? Or did she think she jumped? She wasn't sure.

Jones' name flashed on the screen. *You, you fucked up my silence. It was beautiful until you.* She switched the phone to silent mode and yet she could still see the luminous green light flashing. Ten times or so he had called. Finally, she answered and to this day she regrets that she ever bothered.

He didn't say anything; instead he sang. He sang and he strummed. He sang that fucking song, 'Tears in Heaven'. Barely halfway through, she hung up on him and lay back on the thin mattress with the stale bleached blanket. No tears then. She had used them all up and could no longer feel much of anything. Something changed that day. Something within her had been chiselled off and she had never been quite the same after that. *25 June 2002.*

NEED FOR LANGUAGE

There needs to be a language—
My language
To bear witness to the truth
Of what happened.
Can I hold him accountable
For what he did?
When in so many ways
He had and has no idea
What it was, was
Rape.
Am I guilty for never
holding him accountable
When I had the chance?
When I never went to him
To scream, claw and punch?
When I never went to my mother
Or his father
Or to the police?
When I stayed silent?
All I have now is my memory
Of that night
All I have now are my words

To be a testimony
To that memory that still
Haunts me.

THIRTY-SEVEN

BOBBY-PIN PICTURES

'Given your current situation, we believe it would be better for you to return home to Paris. You would be with your mother, in a safe and supportive environment. It would be better for you. You'll be able to get the help and support you need. And then, when you are ready to return to school, we'd be more than happy for you to start Year Thirteen,' Mr Mandrell intoned.

The girl took it as a very diplomatic way of telling her to fuck off—that was how she saw it. But she didn't blame him nor the others. He said what he felt was necessary to a girl who, short of a month ago, had chased vodka with a whole bunch of pills.

They don't want you here. You're a freak. You're too much trouble. What school in their right mind would want to keep a weak, suicidal idiot who can't keep her shit together? That's why they want you to go home early. It's their way of washing their hands of the psycho girl—that's you. Fucking idiot. You better get your shit together. Those inner voices can be so condescendingly mean.

So, she heeded their advice and returned back to Paris, back to that illustrious city that had been the scene of the greatest crime ever committed against her. She once read somewhere that psychopathic murderers would often return to the scene of the crime and would even attend the funerals of their deceased victims. She wondered what could be said of her returning to a home that was just a few blocks away from The Incident. She felt as though she would be returning to a recurring nightmare that she simply could not wake herself up from. With her mother having no knowledge of The Incident, the girl remained silent. *Bring on the nightmare. Bring the monsters.* Monsters and nightmares don't go away that easily. Sometimes they linger and sink deep into one's psyche for many years to come. Every month or so, the girl would have a recurring nightmare in which she was doing battle with Sultan. Thumping, hitting, gouging, but no matter how hard she would fight him, she could never win. He would always be too strong. He won every time.

Paris felt particularly hot and sticky that early July evening. Thinking her mother would not be home for a few hours, the girl decided she didn't need to cover up her scars with her usual long-sleeved blouse as she had back in the Boarding House whilst she fixed herself a drink in the kitchen. With her headphones blasting grunge music in her ears, she didn't hear her mother's key open the door nor her clanging steps towards her. Her bobby-pin pictures that she had drawn on both arms were exposed.

'What's this?' her mother queried.

Immediately the girl pulled her headphones off. *Shit, my blouse.*

'What?' she asked nonchalantly hoping her mother wouldn't have noticed the bobby-pin pictures across both her arms.

'That! On your arms!' her mother screeched as she grabbed the girl's arms. 'What is that? My God! What did you do? What have you done?' Again her mother screamed but the girl stood there silently. 'What did you do it with? Kitchen knife? What? Tell me!'

Bombardment of questions followed by more questions, one after the other without a single moment for the girl to formulate a response. Eventually her mother stopped. Hand over mouth, head shaking, fist beating against her chest.

'My God. Oh my God,' she cried out.

What the girl really wanted to say was that she could call out to God as much as she wanted but nothing and nobody was going to respond.

'Hair pin,' the girl spoke. 'I did this with a hair pin, a bobby pin.' Her voice a monotone.

'A what? A hairpin? What? You did what? How could you hurt yourself like that? Trying to kill yourself not enough? You do this to me too? How could you do this to me? To your mother? This my flesh! My flesh!' her mother screamed, grabbing at her daughter's arms again, ignoring the fact that the girl didn't like to be touched. 'You did this to my flesh! Why? How? My God! Oh my God!'

Stoicism was not her mother's strongest trait; in fact, one could say her mother had a tendency for the overly dramatic. But the girl simply shrugged. It wasn't out of spite or any malicious intent to be so nonchalant. The girl honestly did not know how to respond to any of her mother's questions.

That night, after the girl had gone to bed, her mother did the same to her own arm—or at least attempted to do so.

'I tried to do what you did. I just couldn't. It was just too painful. You got some guts. So painful,' her mother reported in the morning as soon as she saw the girl.

But again, the girl had no response. She merely stared at the faint scratches on her mother's arm that looked more like the aftermath of her manhandling a cat than anything else. She wanted to tell her mother. She wanted to tell her that when you're that numb, the physical sensation is just that—a sensation. It's something that replaces the numbness, even if it's just for a splice of a moment; and for that moment, the void is filled with a burn, an ache, a rush. And for that moment, you're not empty, you're not void; you exist because you <u>feel</u> something. The greater the pain, the greater the validation of your existence. There is something there, even if it's just a physical pain.

She escaped to her bedroom. The same bedroom that she had crawled into only a couple months ago. She got into the same bed that could not give her solace nor comfort when she had returned home the morning of The Incident, drugged and torn. The girl lay there as she traced her scars with her fingertips, recalling how she came to find the bobby pin as her tool of choice in her vast toolbox of self-harm utensils. The bobby pin—her favourite, a blunt dull ache that set fire to her skin.

The first time she cut herself she was fifteen. Cautiously, she had opened up her lady razor to extract the blade. *Better clean it and disinfect it first; don't want to get an infection.* Yes, of all the things she could and should worry about, getting an infection from her own razor blade was top of the list. She had seen so many films of women slashing their wrists and bleeding themselves out in bathtubs. *Why bathtubs?* She didn't want to die. She just wanted to feel something, anything, but it had to be the right kind of something. A couple of cuts on her right forearm. *Razors cut fast.* Only seconds and the blood oozed out quickly. *Too much blood for such small cuts. This is going to be messy. No, I'm not sure I like the razor. This isn't going to work.* She decided to try a couple more on different parts of her arm. The sadist in her wanted to savour every moment whilst the chicken in her was too afraid she would cut too deeply and bleed out like all the women she saw on screen. She decided to leave the cutting alone for a bit.

In between the razor and the bobby pin, she discovered wrist banging. It was the perfect set up. With the one hand she could bang her wrist against the edge of her desk whilst with the other hand she was able to churn out A-grade essays. Deep purple bruises quickly developed on her wrist, which were soon covered with scabs where the skin had scratched off. Eventually the bruising got so severe that her leather bracelets weren't wide enough to cover them up. She needed something else, something that would give her that rush without killing her and without raising eyebrows at school—just enough for her to feel something, so that she could get through the day. She tried the small vegetable knife she secretly kept in her cupboard. Boarding House rules—no knives except blunt butter knives allowed. A few scratches magically formed on her skin and she watched tiny bubbles of blood appear above them. *Hmmm. Not quite enough.* Next, she went for the standard school scissors but when she considered how unsanitary they were, she thought the better of it so went for the compass instead, not before passing it through her Zippo lighter flame first. *Hmmm. Too pointy. Claw-like scratches. No, that's not it.*

Then she saw it. The bobby pin she used to keep her growing fringe back. As if by instinct, she prised the pin apart, took the sharper edge, dug it deep into her forearm and tore at her flesh about two inches up from her wrist. She still bears the scar. It hurt. It hurt more than the razor, knife and compass combined. Her arm was on fire as she felt the burn race through her, and for that moment she was utterly alive again. She had found her drug.

She soon understood that her newfound hobbies had to be kept under wraps, quite literally. She knew that the bruises and scars would cause a stir at school and that her teachers would get involved. They would ask her if she was okay and when they would see that she wasn't, they'd take her precious pins away. No, she couldn't have that. *No one must know. They can't. They will take your pins away.*

And no one knew. It's amazing how much an innocent cardigan can hide. The girl got away with it for a while until that July summer evening and was confronted by her own mother who was astounded that something as commonplace as a bobby pin could cause so much harm.

Many years later, when the girl had grown into a woman, she caught sight of her mother's forearms. She too had drawn pictures on them, only instead of a bobby pin, her mother used a knife. It pained her to see her mother's scars but at the same time, she felt oddly connected to her. The girl understood that both mother and daughter had, at different points in their lives, become crippled by something that existed only in their minds.

HEALING

For years I would hurt myself
as a substitute,
because I couldn't hurt you.
It wasn't until I learnt
I could fight back
that my scars could finally begin to heal.

PART III

The scariest part of growing up is the realisation that there is no instruction manual to this and that we are all going in blind.

MONSTERS THAT INHABIT MY MIND

There are monsters.

They exist in my mind.

Monsters I call Self-Doubt, Fear,

Self-Loathing, Rage and Shame.

These monsters,

They live with me

And inhabit my mind.

I try to talk to them,

To tell them to

Pack their shit

And find another mind

To inhabit.

But they do not listen.

Rage and Self-Loathing are

Banging on the walls of

My Psyche.

Fear is shaking in the corner

Whilst Shame points at her

And shakes her head.

Self-Doubt keeps pacing

Up and down,

Round and round

In circles,

Asking the same fucking question

Over and over.

These monsters—

They have lived with me

Since I was small and little.

They were small and little

Monsters then.

Now they are big and older

Monsters with cunning ways

To ravage my mind.

I wish they would listen.

I try to talk to them,

To tell them to

Pack their shit

And find another mind

To inhabit.

But they do not listen.

THIRTY-EIGHT

YOU MADE ME YOUR BITCH

She never had a one-night stand with a complete stranger before nor had she ever responded positively to a total stranger chatting her up and inviting her to dinner. Her standard response to any stranger: *No thanks. No. Piss off. Leave me alone. I mean it. Fuck off.*

Up till now, all of the girl's sexual encounters had been with boys she knew. Boys who were friends, boys who were boyfriends, boys who were friends of friends, boys she knew from school. Never a stranger.

She never entertained the notion of going out with a complete stranger nor she had ever been on a 'proper date' before. And yet barely two weeks since arriving at university, the girl was sitting in the Weatherspoons at the O2 centre on Finchley Road with Mr Blockbuster Representative who could not stop talking about himself since the start of their date.

Between the loud clanks of pint glasses, the footie on the TV in the background, the slurred shouts from patrons falling on top of each other in a drunken mess and Mr Blockbuster's verbal diarrhoea, her first 'proper date' felt like a pantomime. All she could hear from him was *blah blah blah blah blah* as she rolled one liquorice cigarette after the other. *Is he just nervous? Or is it something else, like narcissism? Does he know I'm not listening any more? Or am I just that stoned? Ha! What's his name? Something that began with M . . . or O? Fuck. What's his name? Meh. He looks like a Michael. Or was it Michel? This is a terrible date. Will he stop talking at some point? Hmmm.*

A couple of hours later, she was sitting on Michel's divan as she watched him light a dozen candles and play Coldplay on his CD stereo player. Coldplay, or what she dubbed 'suicide music'—music that one contemplating suicide would listen to in order to get that extra push off the edge. But Michel was totally into it, in fact he seemed rejuvenated by it as he sang off-key to 'Yellow'.

To describe the sex as odd would be a gross understatement. Singing to Coldplay songs during sex—all off-key. Mumblings to himself that he needed to 'get deeper' to feel her inside. Then finally after climaxing, retracting to the foetal position and crying. *Is he crying? Oh, my fuck! He's actually crying!*

'It was so good. Oh my God. It was so good,' sobbed Michel, back to her, still in his foetal position.

The girl could not have sprinted out of there any faster. She slid off the bed so as to not disturb Mr Foetal Man, grabbed her clothes and dashed out into the corridor naked. She threw on her top and trousers, stuffed her knickers into her pocket and ran out of there. *Shit, fuck, shit. Don't let him hear you leave! Fuck!*

A big sigh of relief was released as soon as she made it back to her university halls. Straight away she stripped naked and threw herself into the shower, desperate to wash everything about last night off her. With the warm solace of the water beating down on her, the girl began to laugh. Harder and harder she laughed at how ridiculous the whole experience had been. *That will teach you never to have a one-night stand with a stranger, ever again! What were you thinking, you idiot?* She felt like she had dodged a bullet.

But it wasn't over. Only a few hours after her escape, her phone had been blown up with a dozen missed calls and text messages from Michel/Michael-something. She wanted to do the decent thing, she wanted to respond. She wanted to tell him that nothing would ever come of their encounter. She wanted to confront him about the crying. But she didn't. She couldn't. *Chicken shit.* She hid behind her phone, her campus walls and her friends. But she couldn't hide forever because a week later she realised she hadn't returned the *Analyze That* DVD she had checked out. It was now well past due, and she couldn't afford to keep racking up the late fees. *Shit. Okay, this isn't so funny any more.*

She needed a plan. She dreaded the thought of having to go into Blockbuster by herself and confront Mr Foetal Man, who she suspected (not that she was listening to him) was a supervisor thus there almost all the time. Someone had to go with her, someone who would help her feel safe, someone that could perhaps pretend to be her boyfriend. After telling her friend Josh the story, foetal position and all, he decided to accompany the girl to Blockbuster so that the girl could begrudgingly return her DVD.

As she approached the counter, she could feel Michel's eyes burn a hole in her head. She was too embarrassed to look up so with a lowered head, she slid the DVD across the counter, paid the fine, grabbed Josh and dashed out of there. Just as she thought she was let off the hook, Michel called out to her.

'Hey. Hey! Stop! Stop!'

'Yeah?' she said as she signalled to Josh that it was okay to give them some space, but not much.

'Why haven't you returned any of my calls or messages?' He was irritated, irked, angry even.

'Well, I've been busy with uni and it's just been—'

'Bullshit. You just walked out of my room and then you don't even call or message me back? What the fuck?' He was shouting now. She didn't like shouters; it just made her want to shout louder.

'You called me like twenty times and left a lot of messages. That's a bit much.'

'I thought we had something. You didn't call or respond.'

'Look, I'm sorry but that . . . the sex, it was really weird,' she said in a muffled voice, hoping to lower her voice out of sheer embarrassment for him. 'This isn't going to work for me.'

'I see. You know what? You really made me feel like your bitch. Yeah, that's right. You made me your bitch.'

With that he stormed off back into Blockbuster. Josh, who had kept close and overheard their exchange, couldn't control himself as he burst into hysterics. The girl stood there dumbfounded. *That's the first and last time I ever have a one-night stand.*

THIRTY-NINE

ATONEMENT IN WATERLOO

I know how to love you. I have not forgotten.

Ben's piercing words stared back at her from the computer screen. She read and reread the email. Again, and again, her eyes went over the same sentence, over and over. It was probably the most romantic thing she would ever read.

I have not forgotten. I have not forgotten the scent of the rain mixed in with your perfume on my wax jacket nor the lazy afternoons and evenings on the grass thinking ever so highly of ourselves. How arrogantly naïve we were to think we knew something about anything, that we knew about life, about pain, about love—simply because we had read a few philosophy anthologies. I know how to love you. I have not forgotten.

Ben may not have forgotten, but the girl wished he would. She wished she could somehow wipe clean some of the rooms in his memory palace, rooms that contained his painful discovery that she was not who he had so adoringly believed her to be.

Ben's baby face, broken, shattered, screwed-up, ruined. Tears trickling down, lips shaking, pulled tight, jaw clenched. His whole body trembling with rage and heartbreak. All she could do was stand there motionless in front of him and take all the verbal abuse he lobbed at her. She deserved it. She deserved every single moment. She had never cheated on anyone before. A lapsed moment of judgement, the all too familiar smells and tastes, the reminiscence of what was once love for Sultan. A hug, a kiss . . . and then it was done. Sultan and she had fucked. Fucked. Not made love, not had sex, not slept together—it was a fuck. After it was all done, it was evident what emotional sentiment she thought she still had for Sultan was no more than a memory of it. A memory of what it was like before the lies, the drugs, the arguments, the distance, the mess, before The Incident. And there she was, standing in front of Ben, now a broken mess—a mess she had made. She broke him. She broke innocent, kind, beautiful Ben. *You're a fucking cunt. You deserve every single piece of shit Ben hands you. Look what you have done to this poor boy. Hell's made for people like you. Fucking cunt.*

That was over a year ago. A lot of things can happen in a year. A year can do a lot of things to people. She had spent the last eighteen months living in her own personal Hell and lugging it within her whilst he spent the year travelling across Vietnam searching for something he never found. Now both were here, both in London, at the same university. *I need to reach out to him. I need to make amends. I need to atone. I can't keep carrying this around with me. I have to see him.*

After their first rather brief and awkward meeting at the American Sports Bar on Haymarket, they agreed to a more suitable venue: Caffè Nero on Waterloo Bridge where they could abuse caffeine whilst chuffing away on liquorice roll-up cigarettes. They debated the evening away. First melancholically commenting on how London is so much more London when it rains, to how life in the Far East is so much more attuned to truthful expression and living. They sprouted misremembered quotes pulled out of their first-year Philosophy reading list. They didn't think nor feel at the time that they were being pretentious; each merely wanted to prove to the other that s/he had grown, that somehow along the road of shit, they had matured.

It was closing time. Without much discussion she followed Ben back to Stamford Bridge Halls just down Waterloo Bridge.

'Did you know that this bridge was built by women in the Second World War?'

Ben was always full of interesting trivia.

'Nope, no idea. That's pretty cool.'

Armed with beer, whiskey and tobacco, they ventured into Ben's single-sized room—a narrow space of white hospital walls and with too much furniture for you to stump your toes on.

'Have you seen *The Game*? It's an incredible film,' Ben asked as he inserted the DVD into the player.

'No, I haven't.'

'You'll very much enjoy it. I assure you.'

'Okay, let's watch it then.'

Sardined on the single mattress, whose coils poked through the thin cover, they watched Michael Douglas lose his shit onscreen. Not even halfway into the film and they were engaged in a booze-induced debate on determinism and free will. After a few too many shots of whiskey, both concluded that being a nihilist was probably the safest bet.

'After all, does it really matter? Does any of it really fucking matter? I mean . . . I'm studying all this shit at uni, I'm supposed to give a fuck. But really . . . who cares?!' she ranted.

The booze was talking, and it was the booze that dropped Ben's guard as he wrapped his arms around her ever so tenderly as if shielding her from the anarchist demons knocking on her psyche. Nestling his face on her neck, Ben breathed her in.

'You smell exactly as I remember you. Same perfume.'

Butterfly wing kisses. Gentle, soft, tender. Kisses turned to caresses that turned to sex. Gentle, soft, tender—the familiar feeling of being with an old lover. It was safe, comforting.

Post-coital cigarettes. It was sometime after 4 a.m. as Ben played The Pixies in the background when suddenly a tsunami of guilt washed over her. Whether it was the booze, the reunion with Ben or the tragically beautiful music in the background, she wasn't sure, but the whole night left her hollow. She felt empty.

'You all right? You seem disturbed by a terrible thought.'

'No, Ben. I'm not okay . . . I . . . I don't know. I don't know what the fuck I'm doing here. I feel utterly devoid of any authentic feeling, like I'm a minor character in my own TV show. I just don't know.'

Ben took a deep inhale then scribbled something on a piece of liquorice cigarette rolling paper and handed it to her. She looked down at it. It was her name.

'What's this about?'

'So, you don't forget who you are. You are still you. Before, after, still you. I have not forgotten.' Ben smiled and went into the bathroom.

She was immediately overcome with an insatiable desire to run. The voice in her head at first calling for her to run now started to screech full volume: *Get out, run. You gotta run. Get out. Run. Run! RUN!*

Throwing on her twelve-hole Doc Martins and knee-length corduroy black jacket, she ran out of there. Frantic black mascara tears bubbled and burst onto Waterloo Bridge. *This is fucking bullshit. It's 5 a.m. You're alone, you don't know how to get home. You might get stabbed or raped or both. Fucking idiot. How's crying going to help you if you can't fucking see where you're going? Dumbass! Idiot! Keep walking, you've got to keep walking.*

FORTY

UNCONSCIOUS LESBIAN

'You're wasting your time with him.'

'Who?'

'Matheo.'

'What d'you mean? He's my boyfriend.'

'Exactly. You don't need a boyfriend.'

'Why not?'

'Because you're a lesbian and you just don't know it yet.'

'Excuse me? What?'

'You're a lesbian. You just don't know you're a lesbian yet.'

'Um, I'm pretty sure I'm not.'

'Yes, you are. You'll see.'

'I highly doubt it. I mean sure, I can appreciate the female form, but I am not going to eat pussy.'

'Maybe not now, maybe not yet, but one day. One day you will. You're only twenty-one. There is still time.'

'Really? Okay, so one day I'll just wake up and say I'll take my coffee to go with a side of pussy?'

'No, not quite like that, my dear. You're far too intelligent to be with a man. One day you'll understand.'

'But I like men.'

'Only because you haven't been with a woman yet.'

'But I have, and the whole eating pussy thing . . . couldn't do it.'

'See, I told you. You're a lesbian. Anyhow, you're wasting your time with Matheo. He's a buffoon. A man, especially him, is never going to be able to keep up with you, darling. You need a woman to get you, to really see you. Now get back to work, dear, this is luxury retail not a meat market!'

THE ONE AFTER ME

I would think about the one
that would come after me.
I would wonder
what she would taste like.
Watermelon ripened
ready for fingers to scoop out.
Ready to be
Devoured.
I would wonder
how many moons
and stars
you would promise her
as you make her swallow.

FORTY-ONE

THE SEVEN-YEAR LIE

She never had an anxiety attack before, so when she stormed out of Matheo's dorm, shoes without socks, clothes spilling out of her handbag and dishevelled post-coital hair, unable to breathe, she had no clue what was happening.

I can't breathe. What the hell? Breathe. Just fucking breathe. Can't breathe. Am I having a heart attack? Can't breathe. Am I dying? Is this it? This is how I'm going to go . . . on the pavement in Wolverhampton without socks. Fuck.

She was heaving, wheezing even. Mucus and saliva dripped out of her orifices forming liquid threads. Heart pounding with all four paws on the floor, crouching over like some deranged animal. The concrete created craters in her palms and knees. The harder she tried to breathe, the less her lungs wanted to cooperate. Splices of what had come to pass only an hour ago jerked around in the mind. *Crying, screaming, shouting, denying, confronting. Scrunched-up thong buried in between the mattress and wall. A white strappy top. Eyeliner and extra toothbrush by the sink. New shoes, not his size, under the bed. Questioning, denying, shouting. This is fucking ridiculous. Breathe, you fucking idiot. Just breathe! You've got to get up and get out of here, now!*

'Babe! Oh my God, babe! You okay? Fuck! Breathe! Oh shit. Fuck.'

It was Matheo. His mere presence made it worse.

'Please, baby, please just breathe. Come on,' he begged.

When the girl finally regained control of her breathing, she pushed herself off the concrete and reluctantly agreed to return to Matheo's dorm room. She did not want to but realised she couldn't head back to London in her current state. As she followed Matheo back, she thought about what had transpired. She couldn't digest how only a couple of hours could turn her world upside down, how even now, after so many breaches of trust, she still hadn't learnt her lesson.

Matheo and the girl had been together for over a year and whilst she had been warned that long-distance relationships are doomed to infidelity and eventually failure, she decided to trust that their bond would be immutable.

One Saturday afternoon, she decided to pay her beloved Matheo a surprise visit by spending her savings on a train fare up to Wolverhampton.

'Hey, Matheo! What are you up to?'

'Nothing much. Just in my room, chilling. What about you? What you up to, chica?'

'Well, you won't believe it but . . . I'm just walking into your building!'

'What? Where are you?'

'In your building. Surprise! I'll be outside your room in a couple minutes.'

'Wait! What? You're here?'

'Yes! See you in a sec!'

Post-coital cigarette. Matheo blew smoke rings up to the ceiling as she rummaged through the sheets in search for her clothes. White strappy tank top bunched up in the corner. *This isn't mine.* White thong rolled up into a figure 8. *This isn't mine either.*

She had heard the same shit before. The same pathetic lines now repackaged and spewed out of someone else's mouth, but it was always the same, lines like:

- It's not what it looks like, I can explain.
- What? They are obviously yours!
- Come on, why would I cheat on you?
- You're just being totally fucking paranoid. Fucking delusional!

The girl had gone mute from the combination of disbelief, shame and boiling rage. She walked towards his sink for a drink of water. More evidence of his infidelity stared back at her. Eyeliner, extra toothbrush. The girl caught her reflection in the mirror. *Have you not learnt your lesson yet?* Repulsed by the predicament she had yet again stuffed herself into, the girl grabbed her things.

'You're a fucking pig. I hope your dick shrivels up and falls off when you're inside her,' she spat out at Matheo as she stormed out half-dressed and ran out of the building, throwing clothes and shoes on as she left.

That was a couple of hours ago. Now she was back in the same room; the room that not long ago was her haven with Matheo, a place where they melted into each other, where they laughed and fucked. It now felt tarnished, sordid and heavy. Merely being back there left a film of repugnance all over her skin that she desperately wanted to scrub off. Did she know? She believed she did, at least on some level. There was always a twitch in her gut every time she saw Savina and Matheo in the same room. There was always an uneasy awkwardness with their exaggerated effort not to talk to each other, not to look at each other—they pretended to not even know each other but it was overdone. Something had been off.

'Just tell me the truth, Matheo. I can't handle a lie, just give it to me straight.'

She was sat at his desk, trying not to think of where else Savina and Matheo had fucked.

'I'm telling you, babe. Savina was just staying here. I have never cheated on you. I love you. I would never do that to you.'

Matheo knelt down to meet her eyes. He went to clasp her hands. The girl flinched.

'I call bullshit.'

She shoved his hands away and sprung up.

'Stop lying to me like I'm a fucking idiot, Matheo! I know!'

'You're being fucking paranoid. It's all in your head. There's nothing between Savina and me. Stop being so bloody paranoid!'

'I'm paranoid? Really? Sure! Yeah, go on, make me out to be the crazy one when you're the one with the rolled-up thong in your bed.'

She marched towards the sink, sorted out her hair and makeup, put some socks on, then her shoes and zipped up her bag.

'Don't call me. Don't look for me. Don't come and visit me. Don't think about me. Don't even say my name. And what I said earlier about your dick dropping off? I still pray that happens.'

With that, she walked out. This time, Matheo knew not to follow her.

Love, like a bad drug addiction, has a way of holding you hostage. She was the addict and he was her fix. After two weeks of going cold turkey, of countless unreturned calls and messages, she eventually surrendered and answered the phone. But the irreparable damage had been done and after two further panic attacks and a year later, the girl finally gave up. It was time to quit and to carve him—her addiction—out of her life. On the night that she broke up with him, Matheo had gone into a rageful binge of alcohol and other intoxicants and glassed his best friend in the eye. That was Matheo for you.

Seven years later, as she was crawling her way to work, she got an unsolicited monologue confession from Matheo through Facebook Messenger. For some reason he had suddenly felt compelled to offload his sins onto her.

I don't really know why I am writing this. I guess I owe it to you. I guess it's some karmic bitch slap in the face for what I did to you and to others. My girlfriend left me for another guy. She's been cheating on me with that same guy she's left me for. I guess I deserve it.

hat time when you found out about Savina and I point blank denied it, I was lying. I had cheated on you. I fucked her. Whilst I'm at it, you should know I've fucked others too.

I even tried it with your flatmate when you lived in King's X. It was that night you were too sick to come out with us and stayed in. I guess I did it because I was so adamant that you were going to or had cheated on me. I really believed you did. Did you? I felt that if

I cheated on you first, I wouldn't have to feel so bad when you did it. A sort of revenge-cheating, I guess. I don't think I have any excuse really. You can take this however you want but this is my apology.

By the way, I need to know – Did you ever cheat?

Matheo.

She wasn't sure what made her angriest. The fact that he cheated? The fact that he cheated and lied about it? The fact that he cheated, lied about it and made her feel like she was losing her mind for thinking it? The fact that he needed to have pre-emptive in-case-of-emergency revenge cheating? Or that it took him seven years to come clean, and only after he had been fucked over by his girlfriend? But that was Matheo for you.

CONFUSED. EXCUSED.

She had confused understanding
with having his words shoved
into her mouth.
Because only he could understand her
well enough to feed her
with what she was going to say anyway.
She had confused cute jealousy
with checked text messages and examined call histories.
Because he loved her so much
he needed to know where she was
and who she had been talking to.
She had confused chivalry with possessiveness
when he assumed
she had spread her legs or opened her lips
to any man that had spoken to her with a smile.
Because no man could possibly be smiling at her
had she not
fucked
or sucked
or both.
She had confused confidence with him twisting
her arm each time

she said something that displeased him.

And when she said it hurt

he called her a wimp,

a pussy.

Apparently she needed to toughen up.

She had confused patience with him encouraging

her to drown her rage in alcohol

even though it brought out her demons.

Because who else would want her when she's like that?

She had confused his sense of risqué adventure

with being made to dress up and roleplay

as a cheap hooker in ripped fishnet tights

and PVC boots

to be spat on.

And when she didn't want to do it any more

she was called boring

and of not loving him any more.

She had confused commitment with his insistence

that she wore bright red lipstick

whenever she sucked him off

so as to leave a ring of her lips around

his cock

but more so because he enjoyed

smearing her lipstick across her face

like the clown that she was.

Made even more clownish

when she made rehearsed sounds

she learnt from the naked women on his laptop.

She confused concern for his indignation

when a stripper's free lap dance

caused her lipstick to be smeared across her face.

Because it was okay for him

to cock-paint her

but when a woman's breasts did the same

it deserved to be screamed in public.

She had confused passion with degradation

each time he pinned her against the wall

or bed

or stairs

or wherever they fucked.

And when she told him

she couldn't be on her stomach

he brushed it off.

Because The Incident couldn't have been 'that bad'.

Because wasn't it about time that she 'got over it'?

Because when girls say 'no' they really mean 'yes'.

She had confused anger and control with love and kindness.

She had confused.

She had been confused.

Confused.

Excused.

I am not upset that you lied to me, I am upset that from now, I cannot believe you.

Friedrich Nietzsche

FORTY-TWO

THE 5'7 SPERM DONOR

Herman, in his mid-sixties, was exactly how she had pictured he would look. Her mother had stashed boxes of photos—wedding photos, photos of Herman during their years of marriage pre-adultery, and a handful of rare father-daughter photos that were finally given to her when she was deemed 'old enough', which in her mother's opinion was thirteen.

Those precious photos were the only clues the girl had to piece together a profile of a father whom she had not seen since she was four years old. She was now twenty-one. Seventeen years is a long time—long enough for a young girl's imagination to construct stories of and about her father; and while they were not completely fiction, they were embellished tales—a mishmash between fragmented memories, stories her Paupau recounted and those photographs.

But seventeen years is still a long time, and she had spent most of that time fantasising about what this moment would be like: the moment she would come face to face with a man she could legitimately, biologically and legally call 'father' whom she had never expected to be able to find and meet.

After the crushing letters from her paternal grandmother, the girl had abandoned any effort to locate her father. There had been a couple of unsuccessful attempts in her early teens, but the girl had since conceded that Herman would forever remain as 'that man in the photo'.

Around the start of her final year at university, the girl decided to make one last attempt at locating Herman's whereabouts. *If nothing comes out of this then at least I'll know I did what I could. At least I can start my adult life and try to put all that bullshit behind me,* the girl consoled herself.

Using all the personal details that she had on Herman, she compiled a list of addresses of possible 'fathers' that matched his profile, including the address she had of her paternal grandmother in Florida. Then the girl wrote Herman a letter. She explained that she is the daughter he had left in Hong Kong and despite his abandonment, it would be extremely important to her that she could meet him. Anticipating his reservations about her request, she stated she had no intentions to judge his actions and expected nothing from him except to see him face to face. When she was done, she included her UK mobile number, email address, home address, mother's French mobile, Auntie Yin's home and mobile number and even Paupau's landline. She photocopied the letter at her university's Chancery Lane library and sent them to twenty different addresses. *Don't get your hopes up. Even if he does get the letter, he may never respond. Don't get your hopes up,* she advised herself and got on with the rest of the year.

Then on the morning of her final exam, she awoke to her mobile's notification of a voicemail. Still half asleep she played it on loudspeaker as she readied herself for the day. *That voice! I know that voice!* She froze.

'Erm, hi. Erm, hello,' a man's voice with a thick Jewish-American accent. 'Yeah, um, this is Herman . . . your father. Well, um, I got your letter and um, well, I think . . . I think we should talk. So . . . y'know, just gimmie call. Here's my number . . .'

What the fuck? What just happened? Am I hearing this right? Is this real? No, can't be. I must still be asleep. So unconvinced that what she had just heard was real, she replayed the voicemail over and over—five times in fact. By the fifth time she was sure she had lost all grips of reality. *Wake up! This can't be real. You're still dreaming or you're hallucinating from exam stress. Wake up!* SLAP. She gave herself a smack across the cheek. *Nope, I'm definitely awake and that really hurt.*

The voicemail had thrown her off her pre-exam morning routine as she frantically paced around her studio flat. *You can't think about this now. You've got an exam to pass, you can't let this fuck things up for you. No. Get your shit together, girl!*

That was just over a week ago and in that period, she had spoken to Herman a couple times, decided on a meeting and passed on the explosive news to her mother who had agreed to accompany her daughter to the meeting. It transpired that Herman had moved back to Hong Kong from the States in late 1998—ironically the same year the girl and her mother had moved to Paris.

Herman suggested they meet in the lobby at the Harbour Plaza Hotel—a small hotel near Quarry Bay, which is unfamiliar to most Westerners unless there for a business meeting, hinting to the girl that perhaps Herman lived or worked nearby.

She loved her visits to Hong Kong, especially to see her Paupau and gorge on her favourite childhood dishes. But with each visit, she would feel increasingly melancholy, for the Hong Kong she knew and loved was slipping away. Her city was becoming less recognisable with each visit; the uniqueness of Hong Kong with its street hawkers, rustic bakeries, tiny noodle shops and traditional medicine shops were pushed out by jewellery shops, pharmacies, luxury boutiques and shopping centres (as if Hong Kong needed more of those). Signs of Hong Kong's colonial heritage were disappearing too—they were either torn down and replaced as if they had never existed or renovated as superficial caricatures.

Hong Kong had begun to sound different too. Mandarin was heard with greater frequency and in places she didn't expect. *Even the MTR announcements are in Mandarin now. That's weird to hear.* Mandarin had replaced English as Hong Kong's second language and whilst the girl was not so naïve to think this wouldn't happen, she didn't expect it to be so soon.

It dawned on the girl that Hong Kong had moved on without her, or perhaps she had moved on from Hong Kong and in that moment, she knew she would have to accept that she no longer belonged there. She was an outsider and it was not because of her physical appearance, but in how she thought and felt. *Does this make me less Hong Kongese? Have I betrayed my roots, my home?*

'He's here, Herman's here,' signalled her mother.

They had been standing and waiting impatiently at the hotel lobby for over ten minutes. *I guess punctuality isn't his strong suit.* She turned around towards the hotel entrance. There he was, Herman. Awkward, uncertain steps walked towards her. Big, thick thumps that she recognised because his gait mirrored her own. As he approached closer, she couldn't deny that Herman had aged remarkably well, and she could see why and how her mother at the tender and naïve age of twenty-two could have fallen for a man like him.

Now he looked like a pantomime of himself, a man stuck in the Eighties, a wise guy pulled straight out of a mobster film. Dark (most likely dyed) thick curly hair crowned a head with deep hazel eyes framed with heavy glasses. Unbuttoned white Polo shirt with big gold chains that draped over a chest thick with grey hair. Diamond pinkie ring.

'Hello, Herman,' her mother said, stopping him before he could get too close to her daughter.

'Wow! It's you. Oh my God. I can't believe it. You look . . . wow!'

His overreaction made him sound insincere.

'Yes, it's me. This is <u>your</u> daughter, remember her? I leave her with you. Anything happens to her, I cut off your balls,' her mother spat those words like poison. 'You stay as long as you want. Remember, you owe this man nothing.'

With that her mother stormed off.

'Wow! My baby girl! You've gotten so big! You're so grown up!'

Arms reached out to embrace her. It was a hug, a full-on hug. That was the first time she felt a hug from her father that she could remember and the one moment she had spent so long constructing in her imagination. It felt like the worst possible anti-climax. She had built this moment up in her mind so much that she had just assumed she would be overwhelmed with warm and fuzzy pink cotton-candy feelings of being reunited with her estranged father. Instead, she stood there awkwardly frozen whilst being embraced by a height-challenged man who was responsible for half her genetic make-up. She felt nothing. He may as well have been a total stranger from the street hugging her, but in a way, wasn't he? *This is very strange. My father is hugging me. Do I hug back? What's the protocol here? Is it normal that I feel . . . nothing?*

After what felt like hours, Herman finally released her from the unwelcome embrace. There he stood, all 5 feet 7 inches of his sixty-four-year-old rather muscular body. *Yes, he's aged well. Good genes, I suppose. Do I call him father? Dad? Herman? I'd rather call him Absentee Father: Mr Sperm Donor Number 09121942.* She internalised her ambivalence as they headed up to the hotel coffee shop.

'I'm so happy to see you, baby doll. You know your Granny will be so pleased when I call her to tell her I'm here with you. She's the one that told me about your letter, you know.'

'Oh, really?' she said through a clenched jaw. *Which one? The one she sent when I was eleven and said she had never heard of me and wanted nothing to do with me or the one I sent practically begging to meet you?*

'I'm guessing you got a lot to ask me, don't you?'

Eyes not meeting hers.

'Yes. Yes, I do. So many that I'm not entirely sure where to begin.'

Seventeen years is a long time to make a list of questions—there were too many to count—and now they were a jumbled-up pile, a mess, all tangled up inside her, rotting away her sense of self. She wanted to be unravelled, to be ironed out, to know and see where she was really from.

All her life she only knew she was half Hong Kongese, half white. No one in her family was able to give her information further than that. When she asked her family about the guailow side, she was given an array of responses: American. No. Italian. No. Italian-American. No. Jesus people. Yes, Jesus people—that was what her Paupau called her white side.

'Your father, he is like Mr Jesus' people. Like Mrs Mary. Same kind of people. Same, but different. Make you half Mr Jesus people. Mr Jesus people are chosen people. They are special people. Your father, he was always so good to me. He loved me very much, always complimented my cooking! He love my cooking. He showed me how to make guailow food,' her Paupau would recount. Her grandmother had a very poor grasp of geography and all this had left the girl even more confused as to what 'Jesus people' meant.

Her own mother refused categorically to speak about her adulterous ex-husband. The girl had to piece the clues to that half of her identity together all by herself. By the time she was twelve, she had learnt from a Jewish classmate that her surname was actually Jewish, which made her half Jewish too. *Oh, I guess that's what Paupau meant by 'Jesus People'.*

Now as a young woman, she was sitting across the table from Herman, watching him sip his coffee loudly.

'I can't believe I'm here with you, my daughter. I've missed you so much. You know, now that we're back in touch, I'm gonna spend so much time with you. I'm gonna take you shopping, I'll invite you to meet my friends at the office. We're gonna have so much fun.'

Herman's eyes teared up with supposed joy as he pinched the girl's forearm. She was ambivalent towards his exaggerated enthusiasm and then repulsed— the need to recoil, the need to fold herself inwards.

'Herman, if I can call you that. I want to make it perfectly clear that I do not expect anything from you—financial or otherwise. What I do expect is that you account for the seventeen years of absence from my life. It took me a very long time to find you. It was really hard. Really hard.'

Her voice was trembling, anxious that her straightforward, rehearsed speech would cause him to get up and leave and then she would never get the answers she had been waiting for.

'Of course, baby doll. I know I got a lot to make up for.'

They sat at the coffee shop for hours as she lobbed question after question at him. She queried him on every detail and nuance of his stories and accounts. She did not hold back, for she figured this could be her only chance.

When her mouth grew tired and her brain fried, they managed to have something that resembled a normal conversation.

'Herman, I'll be back in July for a whole month right after graduation—will you still be in Hong Kong?'

'Yes! I'll be here. That'll be great! We can do so much stuff together, go out, get some nosh. I'm so happy I'll get to spend time with my baby girl! You got my cell number so just gimme a call when you're back.'

Her mother did warn her that Herman was a brilliant showman. He could turn on the charm, the smooth talk, even the waterworks—the whole lot. Her mother did warn her, and she heeded her mother's warnings, but hope is a dangerous thing. Hope makes you foolish, longing for things that are never going to happen.

When the girl returned to Hong Kong in July as planned, the first thing she did when she landed was to call her father. The phone rang and rang and rang. No answer. She called him every day for the whole month she was there, right up to the last day. Just before boarding her plane back to London, she left him a voicemail.

'Herman, this is your daughter. I called you like you asked. I've been in Hong Kong for a month now. I called you every day. Every day . . . Anyway, I'm going back to the UK . . . I'm actually calling from the airport. Umm . . . you've got my number and Auntie's number.'

The girl felt like a fool with her misplaced hope—like the idiot who keeps going to a dry well to draw for water, even after she's been told there would be nothing there. And there wasn't—there was nothing of substance to Herman's promises of a fantasy father-daughter relationship because it was just that—a fantasy. *I'm an idiot, a stupid, silly naïve idiot.* The girl berated herself for allowing Herman to weave precious illusions in her head and for allowing herself to believe him.

Suddenly the utter disappointment had boiled into pure rage, like a fist from Hell impaling her through her mouth to punch him in the face if she ever saw him again.

Herman, I fucking despise you.

DISAPPOINTMENT

For most of my life
I played out in
My head
What you would
Be like
When I found
You
Until I did
At 21.

FORTY-THREE

AN OFFICER ISN'T A GENTLEMAN

The last time she had to give a police statement was after she had sent a girl in her Sixth Form to the hospital with a fractured skull and broken ribs. *That's what happens when you bitch behind my back for months, for spreading rumours about me, for calling me slut, whore, slag. That's what you get when you slapped me across the face after I told you to stop.*

A plump middle-aged police officer with a thick Cumbrian accent gave her the proverbial slap on the wrist and warned her not to get into any more 'catfights' otherwise she could face being charged with GBH.

'Catfights, they happen. You young lasses and your tempers. We've got matching statements from the other two that it was the other lass who started the fight.' The 'other lass' in question was in hospital. 'You're lucky that both mates told the truth otherwise you'd be looking at GBH. That goes on your record. You're getting off with an official warning, all right, love? That means if you get into another fight, you'll get done for GBH, all right?'

Fast forward to three years later. She's twenty. She's in her store manager's office about to make a very different kind of statement with a very different kind of police officer. The PO looked barely twenty-five and he was what her Paupau would describe as 'guailow ugly'. In other words, too tall, too lean, too pale, eyes too close together framed with thick round glasses and bad teeth.

'You see, too tall. Too skinny means weak man, not good for working, can snap in half. Glasses—may be clever but bad eyesight, cannot see—cannot see, cannot count money properly. Bad teeth mean bad breath, bad breath mean bad digestion—die early. Ah-yah! No good. No good at all!'

Her Paupau had her own special logic, which to the world may have seemed odd or even downright offensive, but the girl trusted her Paupau with her soul and all of her Paupau's lessons stuck with the girl through to adulthood.

'Must remember, not their fault, born this way. They didn't ask to be ugly like this. No one ask to be ugly. No judging. Cannot judge, not their fault, they born ugly.'

It was that reminder that resonated with her as she sat across from the PO ready to give her statement.

She felt like a total badass as she detailed how she caught a known credit card fraudster. A mainland Chinese thirty-something lady had been posing under every single Chinese name under the sun. For months Ms Fraudster had gone undetected with her cloned credit cards and stolen identities, splurging on eye-wateringly expensive goods up and down Bond and Sloane Street. They later found out that her purchased goods were sold on the back-alley Chinese market that ran parallel to the legal-retail street.

How she managed to catch the Chinese fraudster was purely coincidental. In the two years the girl had worked in luxury retail, she had observed the behaviour of wealthy mainland Chinese customers. Mainland Chinese customers can get loud, pushy, irritated, impatient and even downright rude but never anxious when they're about to splurge on £5,000 worth of handbags.

This Chinese woman was different from her legit customers. Something wasn't quite right. The girl felt it in her gut. Perhaps it was the way the woman spoke or her total lack of eye contact, but when the girl asked the woman for a proof of ID to check against her credit card, the girl knew. The woman's eyes darted left and right, her hands fidgeting nervously. Then as soon as the credit card was swiped, it was a 'Code 10'.

'Will you just excuse me for one moment, please? This is very common procedure, just a couple of extra security checks.'

The girl put on her most polite tone and smile as she called the card issuer.

'Yes, I'm calling about a code ten,' she said in her most professional and calm voice.

'Is the customer with you?' replied a woman's voice.

'Yes.'

'Just one moment, please.' The card issuer put the girl on hold and after a few minutes, came back. 'Okay. So, this card has been flagged as a possible clone. You should alert the police immediately and if possible, do not allow the customer to leave the area.'

'Thank you.' The girl gulped, hoping Ms Fraudster hadn't noticed as she looked up and smiled. *Breathe. Just breathe. You got this.*

The girl called the stockroom, still smiling. 'Hi, Manuel, I'm just calling about the last transaction. Yes, that's the one. Could you tell Bobby to code ten it for me, please? We want to make sure all those items are beautifully gift-wrapped.'

'Bobby' was their code word for the police, and she knew as soon as she hung up, Manuel would call the police who were conveniently located just around the corner.

'It won't be a moment, Miss. My colleagues are preparing your items and we're just waiting for your card issuer to lift the purchase limit. May I offer you something to drink whilst you wait?'

Ms Fraudster shook her head and stared impatiently at the door. The girl knew Ms Fraudster would try to make a dash for it, so whispered to one of her colleagues to instruct the security guard to lock the doors.

Ms Fraudster began to unleash a tantrum of Mandarin profanities. It was no longer time to play nice. The girl was worried what the other customers would make of this and decided she had to get Ms Fraudster out of general view, so she attempted to lead her towards the shoe section where there were less people.

'Miss, please sit down,' the girl requested.

Ms Fraudster continued to verbally abuse the girl, gesticulating wildly. 'Miss, sit down!' the girl shouted. The security guards dashed towards them and surrounded the woman, who by now was screeching in Mandarin and in a total frenzy as the other customers looked on in utter shock.

Before long, the police arrived and arrested the woman, who was found to have a stack of cloned cards on her and was wanted for another criminal purchase made earlier that day.

'You did a great job there. We've been trying to catch her for some time,' said the PO who was interviewing the girl for her statement.

The PO leaned towards her, a little too close for what she would consider a professional distance, but she brushed it off as her being too sensitive about her personal space. She figured there was no way a PO would be that unprofessional.

'So, thank you for giving me your statement. That's great. Um, I might need to follow up on this with a few more questions. Would you be able to give me your number so I can contact you, about the case of course?'

She wasn't sure. 'Ummm, you need my number, like my mobile?'

'It's just for the investigation. There might be more questions. It'll be easier to contact you, if I need to ask you further questions, if I have your mobile number. You've been a great help.'

She wasn't sure. It was odd that a PO would ask for her mobile number. She thought surely, he could reach her through the store, but she figured he's a PO. *POs are trustworthy. Just look at him with his shiny badge and uniform. It's just for the case. A PO wouldn't be unprofessional. He can't. He's a PO,* she thought to herself.

'Oh, okay. Where should I write it? On the statement perhaps?'

'No, no, no. Write it here.'

He handed over a flimsy piece of paper that he had torn out of his notebook and she scribbled her mobile number down. As soon as she watched him stuff the paper into his pocket rather than attach it with her statement, she immediately regretted it. *This isn't going to end well,* she told herself.

For the next week the PO kept texting her. First the texts expressed gratitude.

Hello! Thx 4 being so helpful. G8T work!

Then the texts were updates on Ms Fraudster:

Hey gorgeous. FYI credit card lady charged. Couldn't of done it w/out u.

The poor grammar made her shudder. *Hey gorgeous? Why is he texting me like that? It's not very professional.*

Then the texts became more frequent, each one increasingly more inappropriate from the last.

Hey gorgeous. Hey Sexy. How u doin? Wots up?
How's work? Wot time u finish? Lemme escort u home ;) I'll keep u safe!
Cum out 4 a drink

The fact that he was a PO was intimidating. Ordinarily she would have just ignored him or told him to fuck off right away. Instead she sent courteous responses that ignored his advances. She made every attempt to keep the dialogue to professional small talk.

By day eight his texts had become completely inappropriate—he was actually asking her what she was wearing. When she replied,

clothes.

He texted back with,

no, wot you got underneath ;0

This fucker! This slimy, sleazy fucker! she thought to herself, but she was still too afraid to tell him to fuck off. Every time she punched the words into her phone, about to press 'send', she would delete the message. *Chicken shit. You're just chicken shit,* she thought. *He knows where I work. He might even know where I live! Fuck! Yes, but you're still chicken shit.*

She stopped replying, hoping that he would get bored of her silence, hoping he would stop, hoping he would just go away, and she could forget all about it. But some men are persistent. Some men don't like being ignored. Some men don't understand that using their professional title to intimidate a twenty-year-old girl is wrong. Some men, like the PO, his ego bruised, like to take it out on twenty-year-old girls.

> **Wot da fuck? Why aren't u texting bk?**
>
> **Answer bk u bitch! I no where u work!**
>
> **Ur just a whore. FUCKING WHORE.**
>
> **Cock tease. FUCKING CUNT.**

Clenching onto her phone, trembling with rage, she couldn't stop re-reading the messages in succession. *How did I get here? How did this even happen? How did I go from giving a police statement to being sworn at and called a whore, a cunt? Do you know that when you insult me with names like whore, bitch, cunt, you're not just insulting me, you're implicating my gender too? Why sexualise the insult? Why can't you just call me an asshole? That would be better!*

The girl became enraged. *Enough of this shit. Enough!* She felt violated. A police officer, someone who represented authority, moral responsibility, trust, protection, safety—all the things her Paupau taught her that a police officer stood for —were defiled by this particular specimen.

> **I've got copies of all ur text messages. If u don't stop contacting me, I'm reporting YOU 2 da police.**

Ur superiors @ work will find out u abused ur position of power as a Police Officer on da job to obtain my private no# & have been harassing me.

Leave me alone or I will report you.

It took three text messages to be able to fit it all in. SEND. As soon as she did, she threw the phone against the wall. Her precious Motorola Razr phone that she had spent a month saving for smashed and split on the floor of her studio apartment. She was livid. She wanted to take the hammer she kept next to her bed, hunt him down after work and take his fucking jaw off. But she didn't.

Instead, she sobbed all night. She was exhausted, not just from the ordeal with the PO, but from the constant micro-aggressions, the catcalls, the sleazy remarks, the gropes—all of it, by the same men society would have her trust, the very people she was expected to trust, supposed to share her space with. *I hate being a fucking woman. This fucking sucks, being a woman sucks.*

PART IV

When you're an adult, no one is going to make you soup when you're sick and rub your back to tell you everything is going to be fine. You've got to do it yourself.

FORTY-FOUR

UNDER PRESSURE

Scalding hot water sprayed from a plastic faucet over a large yellowing basin. Cheap dishes purchased from the local pound shop clanged together. Adulthood was not quite what she had anticipated it would be, living on a top floor studio in Zone 4; she had a bedsheet for curtains, no proper functioning lock and she had to walk through another family's living room to access her 'flat'. But at least she had her own personal space.

Hands red and raw. Scrub, scrub, scrub. *I'm pregnant.* That single thought shot through her mind as if she had discovered the singularity of existence. So sure, so clear. *I'm pregnant. Nah. Can't be. Can it? Something is off. Something is different. Nothing is for certain until you check. So, check.*

She looked at her watch and it was time to head to her shift selling overpriced handbags in Selfridges. *You're fuelling the capitalist machine with every working day, you fucking sell-out,* she scolded herself. *Maybe, but someone's gotta pay the bills.*

Purse, phone, keys, makeup all thrown into her bag. Door slammed. Elephantine steps thumping down. Elephantine steps onto the bus, onto the Central Line at Leytonstone. Crammed misery on the train and infinite stops, the carriage rocking forwards and backwards, zipping through zones 3, 2, 1. Bond Street Tube. She made a beeline for Boots. *This is so not how I want to spend my lunch money.* Embarrassed smile at the till. *How would I act if I were actually planning a pregnancy?* Pass the Clearblue pregnancy test to Mrs Till Lady. *I can't fake enthusiasm right now; better not to make eye contact.* Elephantine steps thumped down Oxford Street. Staff ID check at the staff entrance to Selfridges. Another embarrassed smile holding back the flush of red as Mr Big Security Personnel Man rummaged through her bag. For a split second they were both motionless. He had glimpsed her pregnancy test. Eyes darted away to hide his judgement. *That's right, look away. Please don't look at me right now. I know what you must be thinking. But no, I'm not a slag, no I'm not an idiot . . . okay, maybe a little, because I'm twenty-two and this shit shouldn't be happening to me at this age. That's right, look away. Stop judging me! You don't know me! You don't know my situation!*

The guard knew he'd found something more explosive than explosives themselves. This was not going to be a good day.

Down the escalators she ran, zigzagging through the hordes and into the toilets. It was time to find out. The instructions which came with the Clearblue pregnancy test made peeing on a stick seem incredibly easy—a simple 1, 2, 3 and you're done. What they failed to point out that there is always a high chance of piss spraying back at you whilst you wrestle with your numbing legs in a squatting position and counting exactly five Mississippi's. It was not her most graceful moment, but there have been and would be many more moments to come. As she nervously unwrapped the test, her hands trembled at the thought that she may really be pregnant. *What if I am really pregnant? What then? What would I tell Noah? How would I even tell him?*

There are few lines in existence that can have such extreme ramifications for a woman, and perhaps no line more powerful than the thin blue line of a pregnancy test—a line that some twenty-two-year-old women would dread. This one did. It was positive. *What? Positive? Positive? POSITIVE?! If I hold the stick at a different angle in a different light maybe it would be different, right? No. No! NO! This can't be right. Oh fuck. This is bad.* She took a deep breath. *But I'm only twenty-two! My life . . . it's just started, I can't . . . I just can't . . . How would I even afford raising a child on this shitty salary and in my shitty studio flat?* Her thoughts were running away from her. Another deep breath. *No time to think about this now. Gotta go to work. Gotta put my face on.*

Trembling, she put on her mask of professional smiles, gave a deep sigh at her reflection and crawled up the escalator stairs. She felt heavier with each step as trepidation of what was to come began to dawn on her.

Stockroom. I can take refuge there, she thought to herself. After convincing her manager that she was feeling poorly and probably should not be customer-facing for the moment, she was allowed to pass some time in the stockroom, preparing the overpriced handbags for sale. Her colleague Mariko-san was doing the same and in a single glance, Mariko-san knew something was not quite right.

'Wassa matter with you today?' Mariko-san's Japanese accent was thick and endearing.

Although the girl was not particularly close to Mariko-san, she felt compelled to tell someone, and the close quarters of the stockroom felt protective. She told her. Without prejudice, without feeling, or crying, or trembling. The girl was taken aback by her own stoicism.

'You must call him. You must tell him. He must know, now,' she instructed the girl as she pushed the telephone towards her. The girl didn't know how she was going to break the news to him. *There should be a manual on how to do this.*

She punched in Noah's digits and as the phone rang, she hoped he wouldn't answer, as if not having to tell him would make this entire shit-show disappear. She wanted all of this to turn out to have been one awful dream. But he did pick up and she did tell him. No hesitation, no umms, no erhs, she just told him.

'I'm pregnant, Noah.'

'Wait, what? What? Are you sure?'

'Yes, I'm sure. I took the test today. I'm pregnant.'

A long pause.

'You can't keep it. You just can't! If you keep it, you'll ruin my life . . . I'd want nothing to do with it. You can't keep it, you know you can't.' Noah's words made it abundantly clear what needed to be done.

It will ruin your life? What about mine? You think I'd want to have a baby with someone who would want nothing to do with it? You think I'd allow an innocent being to be punished for just existing? She was reminded of how Herman had abandoned her, how difficult it was growing up without a father, how her mother had struggled financially and the far-reaching consequences. In that moment the girl had made up her mind and although she believed this was the right thing to do, Noah's tactless words had broken her heart. *I really hate you right now, Noah.*

'You're needed on the shop floor. We need someone to get this sale through.'

The girl knew she couldn't hide in the stockroom all day. *Brave face. Check. Superficial plastic smile. Check. Shoulders out, chin up. Check.*

Bright lights shone out to her as she stepped into the store. Her supervisor passed her onto a prestigiously dressed woman. *Elegance. Luxury. Sell the dream.* And she did. In the next three hours, she sold over £20,000 worth of goods on the shop floor. Her store manager, coming out to congratulate her, asked how she did it.

'I guess I work better under pressure,' she replied with a trembling smile.

FORTY-FIVE

I CAN TASTE ORANGE

'You're going to feel a sharp prick in your left arm. Just relax and count to ten.'

'I can taste orange,' muttered the girl. Eyelids too heavy to keep open.

There was a very distinct smell. A smell she recognised—the smell of disinfected hospital gowns, bleached floors and sanitised surfaces. *Is it over?*

As she came round, she tried to piece together what she could recall, which wasn't much. Her last conscious memory was thinking that the anaesthetic tasted like orange as masked faces with soothing voices reassured her that all would be fine and that she would be out in a jiffy. And now she was in fact out of there, into somewhere else, on what seemed to be a PVC recliner with six other women in identical hospital gowns and blankets.

She placed her hand on her lower abdomen. The area over her uterus felt swollen and tender. She could feel mesh underwear with thick padding between her legs. They must have slipped it on her just after the procedure.

'There will be significant bleeding afterwards. This is perfectly normal.'

She recounted what the nurse said to her that very morning, as they went over once more what was to be expected. That morning she was in fact expecting. Now, she was not.

She looked around the recovery room and observed the other women, all in different states of animation. Some looked ready to get on with their lives as they returned from the toilets having shed their hospital gowns and re-emerged with marks of their individuality. Different colours, shapes, materials and smells. Other women who had just entered the recovery room still looked lifeless as they hung onto the nurses whilst being helped onto their recliners. *I wonder what I looked like when they wheeled me out.*

'Here you are, my love,' said one of the nurses as she handed over a pack of digestives and some orange cordial. The combination made her feel like she was six years old again, break time at school. It was comforting.

'Would you also like a warm drink? We have tea or hot chocolate.'

'Hot chocolate, please.'

'I'll pop some sugar in there too—you'll need the energy.'

She wondered if all abortion clinic nurses were this maternal (ironically enough), this nurturing, this caring. She wondered if you have to have had an abortion already to become an abortion clinic nurse. She wanted to call out to the nurse, to have the nurse hug her, to tell her she was going to be all right. She felt desperate for contact, the touch of a human who cared.

A few hours and lots of hot chocolate and biscuits later, the girl's blood pressure had normalised and she was deemed ready to be discharged. She grabbed the plastic basket of her belongings and made tiny steps into the toilet cubicle. She was nervous. She needed to pee but didn't know what to expect if she were to pull down her mesh underwear. She took a deep breath and slipped it off, ready to be confronted with what was left of her choice. *That's a lot of blood.* The blood was bright, red, thick and had soaked the maxi-pad. The sight unnerved her. Then the pain crept in, slowly at first. The painkillers they had inserted inside her had begun to wear off. Within minutes the dull ache turned into what could only be described as a blender in her uterus that someone decided to switch on. *My freshly vacuumed uterus is now punishing me. You can't think of things like this now, not ever. But it hurts. It hurts so much. This is the price you pay. This was the right thing to do.*

'Is someone coming to pick you up, love?' asked the discharge nurse.

'Yes. My boyfriend. He should be waiting for me at reception.'

'Okay then, my love. Remember, no driving or stairs. Lots of rest and avoid strenuous exercise for a few days. Make sure you read the after-care booklet and let your boyfriend take care of you. You're good to go.'

Small shuffled steps into the reception where she had expected Noah to be waiting for her. *He said he would come. He said he would be there waiting for me when I got out.* No one was there. She looked around, hobbled around the corner. He wasn't there either. *Where is he? I can't believe it. No one is here. He is not here.* Sat at reception, she watched other women walk out on the arms of caring partners or boyfriends, ones who were still in the waiting room when she went in for her procedure. Some with friends or family members; one even had her mother collect her. They all had someone, except her. She couldn't recount a time when she felt more alone.

Thirty minutes later, Noah's black BMW M3 pulled up around the corner. The familiar roar of the engine could be easily detected from the reception. It was only thirty minutes, but it was enough; enough to feel totally dejected and completely let down by the same man who promised her he would be there for her no matter what. But Noah couldn't even get to the centre on time to collect her.

When she got to the passenger door she paused to see, and she was right. He didn't get out to open the door for her. Between the drowsiness of the anaesthetic that still lingered and the fury boiling up inside her, she had smacked the car door onto her own face. It smacked her cheekbone, just missing her left eye.

'Oh my God! Are you okay?'

'No, Noah, I am not fucking okay!'

During this entire ordeal she hadn't cried. She didn't cry when she found out she was pregnant. She didn't cry when Noah told her that keeping the baby would ruin his life. She didn't cry when Noah admitted to her that he had failed to tell her seven weeks ago that the condom had split. Nor did she cry when she realised this entire ordeal could have been avoided with a simple morning-after pill had Noah said something. She didn't cry when she was told it would be another four-week wait to get an abortion on the NHS. Nor did she cry when she decided to tell her mother. She didn't cry when Noah told her he couldn't contribute to the £660 abortion bill because he had 'stuff to pay for'. Nor did she cry when she had to spend her entire work bonus not on the holiday she wanted nor on the leather jacket she had coveted for years, but on an abortion. She didn't cry during any of that. Instead it took a smack to the face to bring her to the realisation that she would remember this day for the rest of her life.

She wailed.

When we are tired, we are attacked by ideas we conquered long ago.

Friedrich Nietzsche

FORTY-SIX

BUSTED LIP AT NW6

'Hello, Johan's phone.'

'Who's this?'

'Erh, who are you?'

'I'm his wife. Tell him his daughter's been crying for him to come home.'

Wife? But Johan said his wife and him have split up? This isn't going to end well. In fact, this is going to end very, very badly. Her gut was knotted. She knew worse was to come and it made her feel sick. This man, this married man—this man who only hours ago had been inside of her, had a wife and a baby daughter. A daughter who probably felt the same way she had for her entire life—abandoned by her father.

Sat in an almost scalding bath, she scrubbed every inch of herself. *Homewrecker. You're that 'other woman'. The woman you promised yourself you would never be. Homewrecker.* Verbal self-flagellation. Ever since she was told her father had a taste for young Asian women and had repeatedly cheated on her mother, she vowed to herself that she would never be <u>that woman</u>. She would never do something like this to another little girl. She had become exactly what she despised.

How could you even have allowed this to happen? He wasn't even your type! She berated herself in the steaming bath. He wasn't her type at all. Apart from his 6′4″ stature, he was not someone she would pick out of a crowd. But he pursued her in his Cary Grant-style three-piece suit and coiffed black hair. He wore her down with his superficial charm, his one-sided smile wrapping around his clever one-liners. He started slowly. Innocent companionship during their lunch break as work colleagues. Before long it was the afterwork drink, then they were having dinner, then they were fucking.

The irony is that she didn't even really like him. She found Johan's obsession with grooming to be tiresome. She was always more of a Marlon Brando kind of girl, but the truth was she simply enjoyed the attention. She liked the affection and the feeling of someone's skin on hers, as any hot-blooded twenty-three-year-old would. And Johan, at the ripe age of twenty-eight, very much seemed like a man. Married and divorced. Well-spoken with a knack for navigating complicated office politics and old-fashioned charm. He felt so grown up and she felt grown up at his side, someone sophisticated and desirable. He was like something out of the film *Casablanca* and she allowed his charm to deafen her ears and block out all her gut feelings to the lies he fed her, lies which she knew didn't quite add up. Lies that poorly accounted for why they never went to his place, why his bank card had a Korean woman's name on it, why he always had to return home at a reasonable hour on weekends.

'My ex-wife still lives in the same place. I just can't find a place to move into right now. It's just easier this way . . . Oh, yeah, well, we have a joint bank account, you know, from when we were married. And we just kept it this way. You know how it is with banks. It takes forever to get bank accounts split! It's just easier like this for now. Don't worry about it . . . My ex-wife locked me out one night when I stayed out too late and I had to sleep at a friend's house. Can you believe that? She's crazy! I don't want that aggravation right now. It's just easier this way.'

Yes, it was easier this way. It was easier to believe his lies and tall tales than to dig deeper, to acknowledge the bitter and uncomfortable truth. She expected it to taste like salty armpits on a humid summer day, but she didn't expect what happened.

'You're early,' she said to him.

Johan was already waiting for her outside her flat. She had requested that he meet her outside her place to collect his things: a couple of DVDs, CDs, a small bottle of aftershave and a pair of boxer briefs. The contents of the dead man's pockets. She couldn't bear to do this at work—too many prying suspicious eyes, too much gossip, too much drama.

She led him inside her tiny studio, took the paper bag from the kitchen counter and handed it over to him.

'Here, now, please leave,' she said with arms crossed.

'You have no fucking clue what you've done,' he spat his words out. A far cry from the smooth charm he had mendaciously put on in the past.

'It's not my fault. You fucked up. I told you from day one I'm not getting involved with a married man. You lied.'

She tried to stay calm, but she could feel her body shake, bursting with adrenalin-fuelled anger.

'No, you fucked up. You answered my phone. My wife's furious!'

'And how's that my problem? You brought this on yourself. You are still married, Johan! MARRIED! With a child!'

'Yeah? Well, it takes a stupid little fucking WHORE like you to fall for it. You young cunts, you're all the same. It was so easy.'

'Get out! Get the fuck out now!'

She started to push Johan towards the door then, BAM! She didn't even see it. Johan had struck her face so fast she couldn't even react. His hand had connected with her bottom lip. Immediately there was the taste of metal, the taste of blood.

'What the fuck? What are you doing?'

She wiped her lip with her hand and showed him the blood.

'Johan, I'm bleeding. What the—'

BAM! She didn't see that one coming either.

'Shut the fuck up! You stupid Chink whore!'

His large fist had slammed into her face, just below her right eye. She had never been hit by a man before and something in her switched. Was it the punch? Or being called a whore several times, or Chink? Who knows? But something switched, just like that from 0 to 100% on the crazy dial. She had been in several fights before—most recently when she put a girl in hospital in Sixth Form, but nothing like this. This was not a fair fight. She wondered if he did this at home and thought again with shame, rage and horror about the little girl left behind.

Standing 5′1″ to his 6′4″, she went berserk. Hammering fists went flying towards him. Futile strikes as he lifted her up and threw her on the ground as if she were a small child. She kicked herself back up to standing instantly, all pain or bruising obviated by a white rage.

'EAT SHIT!' she screamed at him as she grabbed a wooden spoon from the kitchen counter and kept smacking and stabbing him with it.

Punches landed all over her body like lead rain. She had never been hit like this before. She had never inflicted pain on herself like this either. She could barely breathe as he continued to strike her back, ribs, face with his meaty paws. By instinct she grabbed her rice cooker that was still plugged into the floor and slammed it across his head repeatedly.

'Eat shit, you motherfucker! Get the fuck out of my house! GET OUT!' she roared as she continued to slam her rice cooker on his face. As good as the outrage was beginning to feel, it was a relief to see Johan begin to retreat towards the door. As soon as he opened it, the girl lobbed the rice cooker at him, then rushed up to him and kicked him as hard as she could down the stairs. He skidded down a couple of steps before regaining his balance, by which time the girl had locked the door and dialled 999.

Adrenalin, betrayal, pain, fear—all rolled into one big ball of emotional gibberish, lubricated with a healthy dose of mucus, that was now coming out on the phone. Ms 999 switchboard lady asked if she needed medical attention, then patiently took a brief statement and advised the girl to stay indoors and away from her aggressor.

The girl couldn't stop shaking—a mixture of pure adrenalin and fear. *What if he's still out there?* She pictured Johan waiting for her outside her flat when she's all by herself, thumping her over the head, knocking her unconscious. *What if he hurts me? What if he kills me?* She was petrified that she may have unleashed a monster who had no qualms about destroying her. *I need to talk to someone, someone who'd understand.* Suddenly she remembered how her mother had taken on Mrs Whale with a durian. With a handful of ice cubes wrapped in a tea towel against her face, she called her mother.

'Were you scared when he hit you?'

'No. Just angry.'

'Did you hit him back?'

'Yeah. With everything I had. I just went nuts.'

'Good. I am proud of you.'

'But I am scared now. I'm scared to go outside. What if he's waiting for me outside?'

'Don't be scared. I promise you he won't bother you again.'

'How d'you know?'

'Because you fought back. He know you will hit him back. Not so easy with you. You no victim.'

It was not the best time to be out of cigarettes. *I'm not a victim. I'm not a victim. I'm not a victim,* she repeated to herself as she timidly shuffled from her studio flat to the off licence, trying not to jump at every little engine roar or passer-by. *I'm not a victim. I'm not a victim. I'm not a victim.*

REMEMBER

If we do not remember
the harm
done to us,
then who will?
If I don't remember
then who
will remember
for me?
Who?

Be careful, lest in casting out your demons, you exorcise the best thing in you.

Fredrich Nietzsche

EVEN WHEN

she should have seen all the signs
heard all the alarm bells—
the two of them together
a square peg trying to
fit into a round hole
forcing a fit

as he hoped her jagged corners
could be rubbed
and chafed
and sanded down.

but the more her sharp corners
could not be rendered blunt
the more he took solace
in the bottom of an empty
pint glass or bottle.
he knew she is an asshole
he knew she is a cunt
he asked her to marry him
regardless.

she agreed even when
she had recurring dreams
of throwing her jade engagement
ring at him
as she ran through
an abandoned amusement park.

all the signs were there
but she blinded herself to them
she wanted to believe
no matter how mismatched
no matter how brazen
they could work.

even when
on their wedding night
she poisoned her teetotaller self
on sambuca.
even when he would intoxicate
himself beyond the ability
to return home.
even when he ended up
at bus depots or found himself
outside his brother's home.

even when he urinated
all over the corridor carpet
in front of dinner guests.
even when.

PART OF THE PROCESS

'Is this part of the process?'

'Yes, it is.'

'Okay. If you say so.'

So, she ripped off her gangrenous arm and chased him out of her life with it.

Now armless, battered and bruised, she looked at the wound where her arm used to be.

Maybe it will grow back, maybe it won't.

All she knew was how much it hurt and how it would take much more than a pack of smokes to numb the pain.

'It's part of the process.'

'You said that already.'

'So, what are you doing still holding onto that arm?'

With that realisation, she dropped it onto the floor.

'Shame. It was a good arm.'

FORTY-SEVEN

WHITE KNUCKLES FOR MARRIAGE

'Will you come tuck me in?' she beckoned.

'Of course, dear,' he replied dutifully.

Slow sluggish steps towards their marital bedroom. Uncertain steps. Each one would take them closer to the realisation that their eighteen-month-young marriage and five-year-long relationship was coming to an end. They were exhausted from the hours of deliberating, debating, dialoguing, disclosing, delving and dismantling. Exhausted from trying to figure out a temporary solution to a potentially very permanent problem in both their lives. Hugh was moving out for a month or so and they would be able to experience life without each other. They told themselves and each other that this trial separation would bring them back together; that it would help them realise how life as a couple—*une vie à deux*—was far better than two lives lived separately. That was what they told themselves, but deep down each knew that this would be a slow and agonising end to a mismatched coupling that should have never happened in the first place.

To this day she is baffled, not only by how their relationship managed to stretch out for so many years but how and why they got together in the first place. They say opposites attract but, in their case, it was more of a square peg trying to fit into a round hole.

They met when she was still a first-year undergraduate during after-lecture drinks with a mutual friend, but it wasn't until four years later that they got together. 'Leather and tweed' Hugh used to call them, and it was probably the most befitting way to describe them. Tweed: upper-middle class, signet ring, family crest, well-mannered, impeccably behaved, wears brown shoes only in the countryside, always carries a hanky and a pocket-watch. Leather: common-as-muck, foul-mouthed, tattooed, smokes like chimney, abrasively outspoken, unladylike.

Somehow, they managed to make it down the relationship timeline: date, move in together, get engaged and get married. They followed one logical step to the next but had failed to acknowledge the cold hard truth along the way—that they should have probably never have gotten together in the first place. Sometimes the cracks that differences leave are as big as craters and no amount of paving could ever fix them.

Drained, she crawled into their marital bed with its familiar dips and valleys, hills and plateaus. Gingerly he pulled the duvet over her, leaned over and kissed her forehead. Just as he was about to stand up, she grabbed him by the forearm.

'We're gonna be okay . . . right?' she asked with eyes just as bloodshot as his.

She could see her reflection in him. Just as much of a mess. He'd tried too. He looked at her, took a deep mournful sigh and with all the love and positivity he could muster, he told her the one lie she needed to hear.

'Yes, dear, we are going to be just fine.'

She knew it was a lie, and she didn't care. He leaned in to kiss her again, breathed her in, got up and closed the door behind him.

That was the very last time he tucked her in. It was also the very last time he would ever speak to her with any affection or kindness. The next time he would set foot in their martial bedroom would be to take every stick of furniture in her flat. But for now, she knew nothing of what was to come. All she knew was she needed to believe in that lie so she could keep on going, so that she could believe there was some small sliver of hope. *Cling on, knuckles white and bleeding, to your marriage.*

FORTY-EIGHT

NOT EVEN A CHAIR TO SIT ON

Is this what's happening? Do you see this? This is your life. This is your life and it's being taken apart. One piece of furniture at a time.

She stood there and watched as two very large Polish men took instructions from Hugh and stripped her marital home of all the furniture that had been gifted to them at various points in their relationship—when they first moved in together, when they announced their engagement and when they got married. *This stuff is going to make my flat look like a retirement home for rich white people. Am I now supposed to pretend I'm a rich white person?* she thought when her now soon to be ex-mother-in-law had first offloaded their family furniture onto her.

She hated it—all of it—the display cabinet from Hugh's Gran, the grey button-back chairs with the turquoise piping and the matching sofa, the art-deco ladies' writing desk, the gentleman's wardrobe, their marital bed. But now watching them being taken away piece by piece was too much for her to bear, for it truly signalled the end of their marriage.

'I can't watch this. This is too painful. When you're done, lock up and put the keys through the letterbox,' she said to him and walked out.

As she passed the communal skip, she was confronted by images of herself. Photographs of a forgotten past in which they were smiling, happy, gleaming with joy. Photographs that had once formed collages above his desk were now crumpled up and torn, discarded on the floor for all the world to see. *I guess this is what it's come to—our relationship, our marriage, nothing but torn-up unwanted memories in the bin.* Heavy steps marched her towards the gym.

By the time she returned to the flat, every trace of him, of their marriage, of their existence together was gone. All of it, gone. Her flat felt oddly bare, almost anaemic, just like their failed marriage. *You did tell him to come and take all his stuff out. Well good, take it all. I fucking hated the furniture anyway!*

She toured the flat, starting first with what used to be their bedroom—now reduced to a mattress without a bedframe. All her clothes in bin bags with no wardrobe. *Okay. I guess I can live with that.* Then she stepped into the living room, which used to be cluttered with all his family heirlooms and oversized furniture. *The sofa and all that antique crap is gone—good, I hated all of it anyway.* She was glad that her living room finally had enough space to move around in. *Hm, my DVDs . . .* The TV had been left but half of her DVDs were gone. *Fine, whatever, I guess he made a mistake.* She looked around the room again. *That's odd, where's my chair?* She went into the spare room; no chairs there either. *Where are all the chairs?* There wasn't a single chair in the whole flat. *He took all the chairs? He took all the FUCKING CHAIRS! What else did he take?*

Almost everything in the kitchen had remained untouched except for the lemon press. *Really? He had to take the lemon squeezer, the fucking lemon press! He doesn't even know how to cook!*

Throughout this ordeal—the unravelling of their marriage, the girl did not cry, not even once. She didn't cry when they screamed and hurled abuse at each other. She didn't cry when they went for days without speaking. She didn't even cry when he announced that he was going to move out. But it was the sheer pettiness of her soon to be ex-husband that broke her.

Collapsed on the corridor floor, she cried. All the while, a single thought on a loop—*you couldn't even leave me a fucking chair to sit on whilst I cry my eyes out. Not a single fucking chair to sit on.* She couldn't believe it had come to this. *So, this is what emptiness feels like.*

SEARCHING

I tried to look for you
in battery-acid mouths
and coffee breath.
I tried to look for you
in forgotten names and faces
and gluttonous hands.
I searched everywhere for you
trying to fuck out the emptiness
the void you left inside.

GET YOUR SHIT TOGETHER LIST

- *Make list of all new furniture needed*
- *Buy all new furniture*
- *Hire someone to assemble all new furniture*
- *Sleep. At ~~least 8 hours a night.~~ 6 hours a night*
- *Work out how to afford mortgage payments*
- *Unfriend all his friends on Facebook*
- *~~Make new friends~~ Reconnect with my own damn friends on Facebook*
- *Research divorce procedure*
- *Contact divorce solicitor*
- *Make sure can afford solicitor / <u>find way to pay</u>*
- *Learn to eat more than a can of tuna and a carrot*
- *Learn to smoke less than a pack of rollies a day*
- *Get some sleep*
- *Research Cambodia*
- *Tell work about Sabbatical*
- *Have backup plan when things go to shit*
- *Get valuation on flat*
- *Rent flat out*
- *Plan how to store all your crap*
- *Store crap*
- *Leave*
- *Learn how to smile again*
- *Learn how to be me again*

FORTY-NINE

MAD WOMAN LOST

There was something intrinsically off about the person who told her to call him 'Dave'. Something slimy, twisted and warped. 'Dave' with the various pseudonyms and identities that would communicate with each other and access various groups of friends on his multiple Facebook accounts. David talking to Dave, talking to Danny, talking to David talking to Dave. 'David' with the elaborate ex-wife story of bankruptcy, losing his penthouse in St. John's Wood, being sectioned, living out of his red sports car. 'Danny' with the stack of £50 notes in his pocket, beautiful brown eyes and soft-spoken manner. *No. Don't call him.* She didn't want to call him, but she couldn't help it. She was still all torn-up due to her impending divorce from Hugh, and the call to self-destruction was starting to look irresistible.

Her mother had urged her to start casual dating. 'Get mind off divorce. Good for you. Have fun. Go out. Make yourself look pretty. Yes? Maybe you find out what man you want. What good what bad. Try Jewish man. Maybe he understanding you better. Yes?'

She couldn't believe her mother was actually giving her permission to be 'casual'—the same mother that disallowed her from watching *American Pie* when she was fifteen because there was too much sex.

First there was Mr Racist, who argued with her that as she is Hong Kongese, her surname 'Lebowitz' didn't fit her, and in fact she wasn't really Jewish enough to be worthy of that name. *What a fucking racist asshole. I could punch you in the dick. I really want to.*

Then there was Mr Confused, who had recently broken up with his boyfriend and was so devastated by it that he was now questioning everything, including his sexuality. *Poor man, he probably just wanted someone to talk to . . . but I have so much shit going on . . . he needs a better listener.*

Finally, there was a bizarre affair with a Chassid who lived in Stamford Hill, which lasted about two weeks. She found him intellectually stimulating and their hours-long debates exhilarating, until they were at loggerheads about homosexuality, Jewish identity and a woman's right to be a rabbi. *So you're okay breaking mitzvot on pre-marital sex with someone your denomination of Judaism wouldn't even count as Jewish, but you won't even try to be open about homosexuality and female rabbis? Nah.* There was no way she could continue sleeping with a hypocrite.

It was exhausting and eventually she decided she couldn't be bothered. But when David (or is it Dave? Or Danny or even Dan?) left a voicemail inviting her out, she figured as she had nothing better to do on a Friday evening, she might as well give the dating scene one last shot. *It's not like your life can get any more shit at this point.*

David/Dave/Danny/Dan by all accounts (and there were many, many accounts) seemed quite normal . . . at first, but then his charm felt pantomimed and his over-eagerness to satisfy her every whim felt peculiar. His mannerisms seemed like caricatures of actual human behaviour. *He's just a bit quirky, that's all.* She consoled herself, but then after several more dates, David/Dave/Danny/Dan's intensity could only be described as suffocating. On their dates, he touched her constantly—gentle gestures at first, like putting his hand on the small of her back, stroking her arm gently or caressing her shoulder. Then with every date, those flirty touches became greedy grabs which she politely brushed off with a smile. But then when she discovered he had several Facebook accounts with different pseudonyms that would engage in conversation with each other, she had to end it.

'I'm just not in that kind of place right now and I feel you need someone that can give you a lot more. I'm not that person,' she told him over the phone.

'Oh. Okay . . . Bummer. I felt like we were really connecting and getting to know each other, like on a spiritual level too. I feel like I've known you my whole life,' he replied. The ease with which the words flowed made her queasy.

'I'm sorry. It's not the right time. I'm just out to have some fun. Nothing serious, just casual.'

'Oh. Okay. That's totally fine. I hear and respect what you're saying. Just give me a call whenever you feel like meeting up as just friends,' he said and hung up. Again, butter-silk coming from his mouth—he had clearly done this before.

Relief! Not only did it go a lot better than anticipated, she felt as though she had just dodged an emotional traffic collision.

But she couldn't just leave it alone. She had to pick at a nasty scab and call him out of desperation for some sort of human contact, some sort of attention, some sort of anything. It was a pitiful and pathetic call and now she was inside the Marble Arch Odeon cinema.

Synthetic seats—something was prickling her thigh. The thought of having only a thin black maxi skirt as a barrier between her and all those tiny dead skin cells, and who knows what else, made her feel like a hypochondriac. Overpriced popcorn to her left, massive Pepsi Max to her right. She didn't want the popcorn, nor the drink. She didn't want anything except to drill a hole into her soul and hide in there for a very, very long time. She reminded herself that staying at home or spending whole afternoons at the gym wasn't healthy nor helpful. *You can't stay at home or in the gym for ever. You've gotta get out there and at least pretend to be a human being.*

A repulsive hand crawled, like an insect, up her thigh. First tickling her skin through her jersey skirt as another hand crept along her shoulder. *He's got to be fucking kidding me.*

'Stop. Come on. Stop,' she ordered him, pushing his hands away.

'Okay, okay.' He smirked.

Less than two minutes had gone by and his sly, hungry hands had begun to grab at her long skirt again. Gluttonous hands that hiked up her skirt so high and so quickly that she could feel his fingertips push into her. The fear began to choke her and she couldn't breathe. Flashbacks of a dream she had tried to forget. *Not this time. Not again. No. No! NO!*

Rage exploded out of her as she spat at him. 'Stop! Listen, you fucking pervert! Stop trying to finger-fuck me in the cinema or I'm gonna break your fucking fingers! Keep your fucking hands to yourself whilst I watch this film. Now back the fuck off! No means no, you dick!' Her words shot out so fast, like bullets from an automatic weapon, that she didn't even realise what she was saying.

His face registered utter shock and embarrassment. He may have squirmed as he slithered back into his seat, silent as the dead, but it was too late—the damage was done. With a single assault, David had brought her back to being seventeen years old again, only this time she was twenty-eight and should have known better. The rage turned to disgust and then to shame. *You are a fucking idiot. You should have known better. You're not seventeen any more, girl. You did this. You did all of this to yourself. You're a fucking idiot.*

She grabbed her satchel and ran. She ran out of the cinema so quickly that when she burst outdoors, the sun blinded her for a couple of minutes. She imagined the scene near the end of the *Interview with the Vampire* when the sun chars Claudia to ash. *If only.* She continued to run. She ran down Marble Arch and then all the way down Park Lane in her knee-high Doc Martens that began to chafe her feet. Streams of mascara tears painted big, fat lines down her face. Strangers stared. Strangers judged. Faces of concern. As she continued to run all the way home, she berated herself. *I have become her: The Mad Woman Lost—the woman I was so afraid of becoming. I have become her, Mad Woman Lost.*

ENOUGH

For over a decade
I allowed you
to play a recurring role
in my nightmares.
For over a decade
I allowed you
to overpower and beat me
in my dreams.
For over a decade
I didn't allow myself to
win.
For over a decade
I allowed myself to
lose
time after
time after
time.
Enough.

FIFTY

DISAPPEARING ACT

Her mother liked to play what the daughter called the 'Disappearing Act'. More often than not, the Disappearing Act consisted of mere questions slipped into random conversations.

'What would you do if I disappeared? How would you react?' her mother would ask—questions that her mother asked the girl from her teens onwards.

'I'm not going to kill myself. I just want to know if I disappeared for a while, what would you do? If I went on a very long holiday and didn't tell anyone?'

Sometimes the Disappearing Act was just threats thrown in during an argument, blurted out with all the other threats and verbal razors that sliced the girl every time. They were threats of disappearing, threats to discipline a headstrong, rebellious, free-thinking Westernised daughter—threats which the daughter dismissed as a way of her mother trying new tactics to scare her into submission and obedience.

On occasion, when their incompatible worldviews were not only at loggerheads but caused eruptions of anger, conflict and resentment, her mother would really disappear. Sometimes for a day, others for two, but rarely longer than that.

At first, when the rage had settled, the girl would worry about her mother being alone on the streets of Paris. And as it got darker and still no news would come from her mother, her stomach would ache and bloat. And as night crept into the early hours of the morning, bile spewed up as worry-vomit for her mother—an offering perhaps. When her mother returned, there was never an acknowledgement from her side, just a stone-cold stoic face followed by a week or two of the silent treatment. But the daughter didn't care at the time; she was just relieved her mother was safe.

When such incidences occurred more often and for longer, the daughter stopped worrying about whether or not her mother was going to be attacked by some malicious stranger in the night. Rather she was increasingly concerned with a question that no teenage daughter should have to face about her own mother. *What if my mother doesn't choose to come back one day? What then? What would become of her? What would become of me? What would drive her to do this?*

Perhaps they were all signs. Signs that the daughter should have recognised as calls for help. A call to warn her that one day her mother wasn't playing games any more and those threats were no longer to scare her into obedience, submission and guilt. Rather, her mother had really intended on disappearing for good and that question she had to ask herself as to what she would do if her mother didn't choose to come back, would have to be answered.

It did happen. One mid-July evening, in her swanky home in Paris' 16th arrondissement, her mother chose to leave and not to come back. The paramedics said she didn't have a heartbeat for a couple of minutes. They said they had to use a defibrillator in the ambulance. Her mother's method of choice—pills. Lots and lots of different kinds of pills. Pills for depression. Pills for sleeping. Pills for menopause. A cocktail of death.

The girl's mother would later disclose to her daughter that she had even written a farewell letter, the contents of which the girl would never get to read. *Even if you told me what was in it now, I don't want to know. I don't want to know what's in your suicide note.* Thoughts she wished she had told her mother, but it didn't matter any more because to the daughter, the message of her mother's Disappearing Act was clear already. In a world where her mother could not have the fidelity of her husband, she would rather not have life at all.

Love makes people do irrational things and those can be the very things that rupture a mother-daughter relationship. And when that happens, saying sorry cannot mend those broken pieces together.

MOTHER'S LOVE

The moment You
Decided that a
Life without
Him
Was no longer a
Life worth living,
You made me an
Orphan.

The moment They
Resuscitated you,
You returned a
Ghost.

I don't know how
To talk to ghosts.
Ghosts cannot be seen.
I don't know how
To love a ghost.
And I am afraid.

MOTHER'S LOVE

I lost my Mother
That night she chose
Him over
Me.

WE DON'T TALK ANY MORE

At eight years old when I spoke at You
And You did not respond
I told myself You were simply
Too busy
And I should stop pestering You
With my made-up 'sins'
I was forced to confess weekly.

At seventeen years old when I spoke at You
And You did not respond
Even when I screamed for You
To save me from the demons
He left inside of me
I told myself You were just
Another absentee Father
And I your abandoned child.

At twenty-six years old when I spoke at You
And You did not respond
I became convinced
I was speaking to myself
And had started to become
Mad.